Your Words
have power.
Rev 12:11
Terri Shook
2010

Testimonies from the Body of Christ

A collection of testimonies of God's amazing grace

by Terri Shook

Unless otherwise indicated, Bible quotations are taken from

> The King James Version. Copyright © 1976 by Thomas Nelson, Inc.
> The New King James Version. Copyright © 1997 by Word Publishing.
> The New International Version. Copyright © 1973, 1978, 1984, by International Bible Society, Tyndale House Publishers, Inc and Zondervan Publishing House.
> The Message Version. Copyright © 1993, 1994, 1995, 1996, 2000, 2001, 2002 by NavPress Publishing Group.

www.xulonpress.com

Acknowledgements

Although my name appears as the author of this book my contribution was very small.

Several years ago, I was inspired to put a book of testimonies together but like so many things I never got around to it. Well, now I see that God had a plan all along. So when my friend Tamara Berry asked that I pray about doing a fundraiser for her son Taylor, I was ready before she finished the sentence.

Inspiration and divine guidance worked together in the Body of Christ to produce this book. Each person who answered the call and submitted a testimony did their part. I can't thank them enough. Without their thoughtful submissions we wouldn't be writing this acknowledgement. God has a plan to use your words of praise. And your gratefulness for His mercies is pleasing to Him.

I knew all along that the book title would be *Testimonies from the Body of Christ*. One day Sylvia Ramsey came to our weekly accountability meeting and said "God made me get up and paint and this is what happened!" Lo and behold, the book cover was born.

Then my dear sister/friend, Donna Linnane said to me, "I want to be your editor". I had no idea at the time, what a gift that would be. But as the days went by I began to appreciate God's plan for her to walk through this with me more than words can tell.

Next God's plan was for us to have a cheerleader and Gail Anderson answered that call. She was tireless in asking, reminding, and asking again. Going the extra mile in convincing people to get on board with this effort is what has made this book the blessing that it is.

All along the way the Body of Christ has prayed, encouraged, spoken Holy Spirit wisdom, passed emails, given us free advertising, and on and on it went until the job was done. This has been one of the most amazing experiences of my life. It was something like being on the front row of a "God Concert" watching in amazement as He orchestrated each and every move.

What else can I say but "Thank you GOD"!

Terri Shook

Foreword

In Sept. of 1999 Taylor was diagnosed with a rare heart disease called Restrictive Cardiomyopathy. Restrictive Cardiomyopathy is a rare form of heart muscle disease that is characterized by restrictive filling of the ventricles. The inability of the heart to relax and fill with blood results in a "back up" of blood into the top chambers of the heart, lungs, and body causing heart failure. Restrictive Cardiomyopathy occurs in only 5% of all cardiomyopathy cases; approximately one in every million children develops Restrictive Cardiomyopathy.

In May of 2000 Taylor underwent his first cardiac transplantation at Texas Children's Hospital in Houston, Texas. At this time the only form of treatment available for children with this disease is cardiac transplantation.

Taylor had a difficult time his first year post-transplant due to multiple episodes of rejection. He is prone to upper respiratory, viral, and bacterial infections due to the fact that he takes four immunosuppressant drugs,

Taylor is seen every six months at which time he undergoes a cardiac catheterization and right ventricular biopsy to ensure the health of his new heart. At our last visit Taylor was placed on restriction of strenuous exercise. He was found to have a right atrial enlargement and right bundle block. He has thousands of fistula branches from the left coronary artery to the left ventricle and from the right coronary artery to the right ventricle.

Taylor has enjoyed a normal life over the past nine years. He has played soccer, baseball, and swam for the Club Estates Marlins. He has been given the opportunity to go to school and receive an education despite frequent illnesses caused by taking post transplant drugs.

Because of the side effects of so many transplant drugs and the damage done from repeated episodes of rejection children with heart transplants require a second and sometimes a third cardiac transplantation within the first ten years. We have been blessed to have our first transplant last nine years, and to only have just begun to experience the difficulty that arises from numerous infections, episodes of rejection, and immunosuppressant drugs which will require us to get a second cardiac transplant in the future.

The profits from this book will help pay for expenses incurred that are not covered by medical insurance for that transplant.

"We need the community of faith, the body of Christ. We need other sisters and brothers who love us, support us, and give us their discernment. And we need to be connected to the heavenly community of the past—"the communion of saints." We are empowered by learning their stories, sharing their struggles, gaining strength from their courage, learning from their mistakes, and being instructed by their teaching."

Richard J. Foster, Streams of Living Water

THE FULLNESS OF HIS GRACE

One blessing after another
Washes over me -
Like waves upon the shore
And yet I fail to see.

I cry, "Where are you Lord?"
While you are near to me -
Oh Lord, dear Lord
Open my eyes to Thee.

As I awake from slumber
A gift is awaiting me -
Another day of precious life
To live my destiny.

One blessing after another
Washes over me -
Like waves upon the shore
And yet I fail to see.

I cry, "Where are you Lord?"
While you are near to me -
Oh Lord, sweet Lord
Open my ears to thee.

You bring those into my life
That only I can touch -
Some may be desperate and
Others not needing so much.

One blessing after another
Washes over me -
Like waves upon the shore
And yet I fail to see.

I cry, "Where are you Lord?"
While you are near to me -
Oh Lord, precious Lord
Open my heart to thee.

Rita Ramsey
11-06-04

I find one of the wondrous things of the Bible is KNOWING that it is the inerrant word of God. No words are accidents. In John 1:16 it says that we have ALL received one blessing after another. Not some of us, but ALL of us. And how true those words are and have been in my life.

It should be easy for all of us to look back through our lives and see God's hand. Unfortunately, so many times in life we wonder where God is when the things that we desire do not happen. I believe that there will always be things we will never understand, this side of heaven.

But I also believe that there are so many good things that happen in our lives and yet we never cry out "why me, Lord?" We never cry out "Thank you, Lord, for blessing me!" The good things we seem to credit to OUR intelligence, good fortune or hard work. Why is that?

For my life, one of the Lord's greatest blessings for me has been that His mercies are new each day. Remember the parable of the two men who each owed a debt? The question was "who will be more grateful that the debt was forgiven - the man whose debt was great or the man whose debt was small? The answer is - the man whose debt was great.

My debt was great. My sins were great. My shame was great. The pain I caused others and myself was great. When I was unable to forgive myself, the Lord reached down into my pit and pulled me out. I came to understand that He has loved me unconditionally since He knitted me in the womb. He knew and loved me before my sin; during my sin and after my sin. What an amazing thought that nothing I could do would make my Lord love me less and nothing that I could do would make my Lord love me more.

I am painfully aware that I have broken my Lord's heart, and my prayer is to make my Lord smile for my remaining days. My prayer is that the lord will open my eyes to those in need; open my ears to those crying out in pain; and to open my heart to those who feel unloved or lost in that pit.

Thank you, Lord, for another day to live out my destiny and to accomplish those things that you ordained for me to accomplish before I was born.

Rita Ramsey

There's Even Room for Me

"…there is no difference, for all have sinned, and fall short of the glory of God." Romans 3:22-23

Today, it seems almost silly to me. For years… literally, for years…I believed that I had no testimony. I knew that I was called to be a witness, that scripture was readily available to read, and the Great Commission to go to all the world and teach about Jesus was well known to me. I had no trouble believing and understanding that a commitment to live for Jesus includes a commitment to tell others about Him and why I have put my faith in Him. I just believed that I had to use the life of other people as an example when I spoke about the power of the Lord to change people. I believed the testimony of others was the best way to illustrate the saving grace of God. I believed that if I told my story… no great message would be delivered…and no great result for God would be experienced. I therefore believed that I had no testimony of my own.

You see, my great-grandfather was a Baptist minister. He founded a church in Bryan, Texas, and oversaw the construction of the first building for the family of believers he organized under the power and direction of the Holy Spirit. Primera Iglesia Bautista in Bryan, Texas has a building which still bears his name today, some 100 years later. My grandfather was reared to be a servant of God, and my father was reared in the same manner. I was attending church weekly as I was being developed in my mother's womb. All my life I had been taught scripture and lessons of God's Holy Word. I never sampled alcohol, drugs, or even cigarettes when I was a young boy or even a teenager. I never spent time around those who did use those vices. I did not spray-paint the property of others, and I did not even hang out late in the night with young people who did not attend church. I was a "goody two-shoes" to the max, and that was all I ever was.

It is because I never had a "road to Damascus" experience that I thought I had no testimony to deliver. Even after taking leadership roles in church as a young man who had graduated from college a few years earlier, I still believed that I had no testimony of my own. I almost envied those who had been delivered from a life of crime or substance abuse, because their testimony was so very powerful and demonstrated a miraculous change of life, empowered only by the Holy Spirit of God.

One day, it was the simple lyrics of a song that changed my belief of testimonies, and changed it forever. The simple lyrics talk about how the ground is level at the foot of the cross and we all are equal in the light of the cross; for the love of God is given freely to all because the ground is level, at the foot of the cross. For some reason I did not understand, the words of Paul in Romans, Chapter 3 became suddenly clearer than ever before: *"for all have sinned and fallen short of the Glory of God."* I was included in the word "all," and despite my "goody two-shoes" upbringing, I had fallen short of His Glory. Without the blood of Jesus, my sin would still be exposed. It mattered not at all that my sin did not include crime or substance abuse: sin is still sin. I am blessed, however, because the grace of God is greater than all my sin; and it is greater than yours, too.

After the mission of Jesus on Earth was finished, God had another mission for him. He was to use His carpenter skills in a new, Heavenly setting. Jesus was to construct our eternal home with Him. We read in John 14: 2 -3:... *I am going there to prepare a place for you. And if I go to prepare a place for you, I will come back and take you to be with me that you also may be where I am.* Even I, a goody two-shoes, have a testimony. I once was lost; but now, I am home-sick...homesick for a place I've never been. One day, I'll fly away, to a land where joy shall never end. While I am here, however, I shall tell the world that He's my savior.

Jonathan Ibarra

God is Real

It is always wonderful to be able to tell people about how God works, not only in my life but also in the lives of so many. When I was 37 years old, my life was good, probably better than that of most people I knew. I had a wonderful, dedicated husband, the sweetest son a mother could ask for, and I was the owner of a successful small boutique. The outside of my life looked great, but the inside was full of hurt, grief, despair, and deep depression and nobody knew. I felt so alone, so lost and so tired. I did not know God or His wonderful son Jesus; you see, I grew up in a cult.

When I was 7 years old, I was invited to Vacation Bible School. Afterwards I went home, zipped up my new Bible and washed it, not knowing that this would ruin it. My mother said that she could replace it by calling one of our cousins. My cousin brought over a different kind of Bible, and from that time forward we were in the cult. Because my mother did not know Scripture, it was very easy for her to be deceived. The Bible tells of this happening over and over again. 2 Timothy 3: 1-7, *"But understand this, that in the last days there will come times of difficulty. For people will be lovers of self, lovers of money, proud, arrogant, abusive, disobedient to their parents, ungrateful, unholy, heartless, unappeasable, slanderous, without self-control, brutal, not loving good, treacherous, reckless, swollen with conceit, lovers of pleasure rather than lovers of God, having the appearance of godliness, but denying its power. Avoid such people. For among them are those who creep into households and capture weak women, burdened with sins and led astray by various passions, always leaning and never able to arrive at a knowledge of the truth."*

When a mother gets captured, so does her children! So I grew up in a works-based religion, always working and trying to get God's approval but never feeling His love for me. I did this for years. I did not have Christmas, celebrate birthdays, salute the flag, go to football games, go to pep rallies, or have any close friends. It seemed that this is what God wanted me to do, and I so wanted to please Him. But when you try to earn God's love you just never know how much work you have to do. I worked and worked and worked some more for God. I never felt His love or His presence. Finally at the age of 17, I just gave up. I gave up on God, quit going to the cult, and avoided all association with other members. Nor did I try to find God on my own, because we were made to believe that He could only be found through the cult and no where else.

I isolated myself and begin to live my life without religion. I married and had a beautiful son. Five years later my marriage was in trouble and we separated. During the separation, my husband died in an accident. I was 23 years old and I felt so alone again. I remarried to a wonderful man who said that he was a Christian, a follower of Christ. He was a great husband and a good father for my son (we just celebrated 30 years of marriage). Early in our marriage he tried to tell me about his God, the God of the Bible, the God who has a son named Jesus. I would not have it and did not want to hear about his God. At this point in my life I did not even know if God existed and if He did, I wondered, why didn't He help me?

I opened a small boutique with my family, and things appeared to be going well, except that I was becoming more and more depressed. I worked hard all of my life and was so disappointed. I began to feel that this was just the way it worked. You were born, you worked hard and then you died. I think that I would have tried to die, but I felt that I would have been disappointed in that also. One day my thoughts turned to prayer. I thought I would pray to the God my husband knew, but I did not know how to pray. So I decided to pray this: **"God, I need to know two things; I need to know that you are real, and that you hear me."** I prayed hard for months; I prayed going to work and coming home. One day I went to the office in the worst state of mind; I remember telling my mother that I did not want to see anyone. Three minutes later she knocked on my door and announced that a lady wanted to see me. I let this young woman into my office expecting to hear another sad story about her life and how she needed my help. But surprisingly, this is what she said, **"I was going to Del Mar College this morning when God spoke to me and sent me to this boutique with this message. God wants you to know that He is real and that He hears you. Your prayers have been answered"**.

God had heard me. This was mind-blowing. What was I to do with this information? It took me a couple of months to think about what God had said to me, and one day I was in a bookstore looking for more self-help books when the thought occurred to me to buy a Bible. So I bought one that is designed to be read in a year. I began reading Genesis, and was amazed to find out that the characters in Genesis were sinners, but God still loved them. Despite all their mistakes, all their wanderings, and all their wrong decisions, God still loved them. He pursued them and desperately wanted to have a relationship with them. Not a religion, but a pure one-on-one relationship of goodness and love. I wanted that too! I wanted to be loved like that. I wanted to know that God loved me too!

I kept reading. I went to the book of John in the New Testament and I fell in love with Jesus, God's only begotten son. I realize that it was through Jesus that I could get God's love. John 10:30 tells us *"I and my Father are one"* and then John 3:16 tells us *"For God so loved the world that He gave His only begotten Son, that whosoever believes in him should not perish but have eternal life."* Oh, how my eyes were beginning to open and my heart beginning to heal. God loving me right there in the Bible. How was I going to show Him that I loved Him back? And then I read John 14:6 *"Jesus said to him, "I am the way, and the truth, and the life. No one comes to the Father except through me."* It was that easy: love the Son. I love the Son, and I have been falling in love with the Son more and more every day of my life.

The Holy Spirit tells us in Romans 10:9 *"If you confess with your mouth that Jesus is Lord and believe in your heart that God raised him from the dead, you will be saved".* I confessed Jesus as my Lord and Savior; my life has changed from depression to deliverance, from being lost to being saved, from hopelessness to joy. I was born again, praise God.

My favorite verse is found in Romans 8:38 *"For I am sure that neither death nor life, nor angels nor rulers, nor things present nor things to come, nor powers, not height nor depth, nor anything else in all creation, will be able to separate us from the love of God in Christ Jesus our Lord."*

Saved by grace not by works,

Debbie Salge

God Can Make a Way

A few years ago I joined a medical mission team that would travel to Mexico and conduct medical clinics to treat the people who lived in the colonias and in the little villages. The people we served were extremely poor, many living in cardboard huts. This medical team and others from the states were the only form of health care that the people in these areas would receive.

Each time I went I was truly blessed. The team would see patients from early morning to late in the evening for the three days we were there. We would treat anyone that we could, who came into the clinic. Most of the people that came had the general run-of-the-mill illnesses: common cold, high blood pressure, diabetes etc.

One day when I was working in the admission clinic in Mexico, a little boy stood straight and tall in front of me. He was a dear, dear little boy. His mother was with him. He was trying to be as brave as possible and I fell in love with him immediately. As I spoke to him, I put my hand on his head and then on his neck trying to reassure him. As I ran my hand over this little guy's neck I felt a large lump under his chin. It looked like the mumps. But the lump was only on one side. On that particular day we had a pediatric surgeon from Driscoll Hospital volunteering in the clinic. I asked the doctor to look at the little guy. When the little fellow was examined it was determined that this lump was in fact vascular and it was a vein that could rupture at any time. Rosendo was seriously ill.

The opportunity for Rosendo to have surgery in Mexico was nil. The family was very poor and could hardly afford food. As a team we prayed for this family and for Rosendo. Our prayer was for God to make a way. It is extremely difficult to get care in Mexico if you are poor and even more difficult to get care in the United States if you are not an American citizen. Just getting Rosendo across the Mexican border seemed impossible.

As the saying goes and as I know for sure, "We serve an awesome God"! Not only did God make a way for Rosendo to cross the border, he opened a way for Driscoll Children's Hospital to perform the intricate surgery. The Lord also provided homes for Rosendo's parents to stay in during the surgery and for the period of recovery. The Lord provided the total package.

Working as a Registered Nurse in the health care field I have been given many opportunities to see the magnificent hand of God on and in people's lives. Many times while working I did not even acknowledge how the Lord touches our lives or how present He is.

It took a trip with a mission team and a wonderful little fellow named Rosendo to bring me to the full realization of the wonderfulness of our God and how He is with us always.

The team's prayers were answered....in many more ways than we imagined.

Anonymous

Expecting God for the Rest of the Story

G od healed my heart and called me to be His witness. It happened in 1995 when I was in the emergency room with a racing heart rate...220 beats per minute. The nurses were getting ready to attempt starting an IV for the third time when I asked if I could pray for them. I knew that under that very professional façade were two nurses who were terrified that they'd stick me again and still not get an IV line started. I prayed and thanked God for their skills and asked His blessing upon all of us. My pulse jumped to normal which was about half of where it had been! There was no need to start an IV and word spread throughout the hospital. That day a doctor happened to be in the hospital. He used to come to Corpus Christi once or twice a month as an excuse to fly his jet airplane. He stopped by to tell me he could fix my problem. I had an extra electrical impulse that caused my heart to beat too fast. He had done the same procedure on basketball player Hakeem

Olajuwon. The procedure was called a myocardial ablation. This ablation was a quick procedure where he nuked the nerve that was stimulating my heart to beat fast. I love that OBLATION is what I thought it was called. Oblation is a gift, as I had often heard as part of the Eucharist, as "a full, perfect and sufficient sacrifice oblation and satisfaction". This certainly was a gift and I have a perfectly healthy heart as a result and am so grateful. I decided to witness to those who had a reason to know this story.

Every time I have had blood drawn, I have told that story to the phlebotomist and asked his/her name and prayed for a successful blood draw and for God's blessings on my technician. The first time I told it, I was a little chicken; each time it gets easier. I can testify to God using what might have been meant for evil to be used for good. I have lousy veins; my mom has worse ones. It used to be that there would always be several attempts to get a small vial blood sample. Since that time I have not needed to be stuck more than once with one exception. Recently, I was at the doctor's office and told my story and he went to draw blood and he did not get in a blood vessel. I asked him if something was going on in his life that he needed proof that God loved him and he said he was struggling with several things. I didn't ask for specifics but prayed again and asked God to show up and show off to be a proof for him that God was real and had a plan and purpose for his life. BINGO! Later that day I ran into the doctor who employs that young man and shared what had happened, and told him that I really enjoyed the whole experience. This doctor is one of my favorite people, but being a good person doesn't get you to heaven (but it does make the world a nicer place). My prayer for years has been that he will know Christ as his personal savior. I'm expecting God to do the "rest of the story!" and get my friend to heaven. Even if I have to be stuck like a pin cushion, I'd do it!! May God use this experience to His Glory.

Linda Pate

Thanks for the Light

When I was a young boy, my parents sent me to a Catholic school. I was taught from the beginning that Jesus was like a big brother and I could ask him for anything. It wasn't like we were a real religious family, but we tried to do what was right. As far as the Bible went, we had one. My parents led me to believe that the Bible message was that God loves all of us a lot. That was good enough for me. At that age my parents knew just about everything so when they told me stuff, I pretty much believed them.

On Sunday night the family was gathered around the TV to watch "The Wonderful World of Disney". Mom would pop a big bag of popcorn, and all of us would settle in for the movie. Well, during the movie I had gotten thirsty and asked if someone would turn on the light in the kitchen so I could get a drink of water. You see we were in the front room with the lights out because the program looked better with the lights out. The kitchen was through the completely dark living room and at the other end of the house. No one wanted to go with me, because they were all interested in the program. I wasn't tall enough to reach the light switch, but wanted a drink to wash down the salty popcorn.

Finally, when no one would go with me, I headed off on my own. At the edge of the next room, where the light from the TV stopped illuminating my way, I stopped and asked one more person to go with me. At age 5 it seemed the natural thing to do. I lifted my left hand way up in the air and asked Jesus if He would go with me. I can't say that I felt Him holding my hand, but I believed that He did. I walked through the first room and into the kitchen turned left to where no light from the house could reach. But as I did, centered in the window over the sink, was a full moon lighting my way. I put my hand down, got my drink, smiled at Jesus, and told Him "thanks for the light." I was sure that He had pushed it into position just for me.

Ed Schetzsle

God Heard

A few years ago my son succumbed to the pressure of three kids, a wife, work and going to school for his masters. An emotional wreck, he was hospitalized for observation. As I processed everything that happened that week I found myself wandering the house and effectively lost.

Finally at about 3:30 PM I went to my bed, lay face down and began to pray. As I lay there I could imagine my son lying in a hospital bed in the same position, crying. I began to petition God to enter into his suffering and make his presence known. So I continued to pray but found after only a few minutes that I could pray no more. I got up wandered the house for a while and then went to my Bible study and there it was.

I was doing a daily Beth Moore study on the Patriarchs. As I opened up the study to "Day Three," I noticed a picture of a small boy in the right hand margin. Under the photo was the scripture, Gen. 21:17, *"God has heard the boy crying,"* I was so thankful to read that, I can not put into words how that scripture comforted me. And then there was more,

The study is at the part in Gen. 21 where Sarah has insisted that Abraham send her maidservant Hagar and her son Ishmael away. Abraham is between a rock and a hard place. This is Abraham's son. So off Hagar and Ishmael go into the desert. Soon the water runs out and Hagar places her son under a bush to die while she walks several yards away and waits. She has forgotten that God has a plan for Ishmael. In chapter 16, an angel of the Lord told Hagar that He would increase her descendants and that they would be too numerous to count. But God hears the boy cry and reveals himself to Hagar again. A well is just yards away giving the life-giving water. He drinks and lives and God was with him as he grew up.

God sent my son into a desert, but he was not alone either. God heard the boy cry and the Well is always nearby with that "life-giving water". I rested in God's promises that day, and I know God has a plan for his life.

Anonymous

A Mother's Gift

I will never forget the day I met Taylor Berry, a little boy with a head full of curly blonde hair, big blue eyes and an appetite for sports, as if that would be his lifelong ambition. But I didn't think it would be just a dream, because he had more talent in his little pinky than most athletes I knew.

He followed around behind my son, who was 5 years older than he was, and looked up to him as a mentor. Despite the age difference, they got along great.

Because we were across-the-street neighbors, we saw a lot of Taylor. There were several of us, as neighbors, who got together after work on the driveway to watch the kids play. We didn't realize that we would soon have to fear for Taylor and his family.

When Taylor was 5 years old, we received the news that he would need a heart transplant. I was devastated. I couldn't imagine what his family must be going through. It was more than I could handle. But I was determined to be supportive and do whatever I could do.

In a matter of days, Tamara was packing the family to move to Houston. The only thing I could think of to help was to visit them in Houston. So, I packed up my kids and we would drive to Houston to stay the weekend and provide some sort of support in the midst of all this fear of the unknown.

I can remember on one occasion while we endured the endless waiting in the hospital, Taylor and my son decided to play a game where they hid his pee container. Taylor was just relieved to have my son there to keep him company.

Although I was not part of the heart transplant process, my heart ached for Tamara, as the mother of this vivacious little boy, and the fear she must be experiencing.

When they finally arrived back in Corpus Christi, I took Taylor on several occasions to run errands with me, or just to hang out. Although he had to wear a mask on his face, he seemed overjoyed to be back home with his friends. He was uncomfortable with the stares and questions about his mask, but he seemed to take everything in stride. I was proud of this little boy wonder and wanted to show him off. I can remember him and my son playing softball in my front yard with his mask on!!

Taylor often spent the night with us, but this one particular occasion changed my life. I was oblivious to what it takes to care for a child that had undergone this surgery, and just wanted to give Taylor anything that made him happy. What made him happy this particular night was macaroni and cheese. Easy enough. I made a huge serving of it. Little did I know that he wasn't supposed to have salt.

The next morning when I woke him to take some pill that was required, his body decided to have a seizure-type of occurrence. It was short-lived, but his body stiffened straight out and shook uncontrollably as I instinctively put my right elbow on his chest and my other arm on his leg to flatten him out and hold his body down. As his body responded and became calm, I looked at his face. With terror in my soul for what I had just experienced, I looked in his eyes only to see him smile back at me and peacefully close his eyes and go back to sleep.

How blessed I felt to have this boy STILL in my life after all that had happened. It was then that I knew that no matter what happens to my children or me, we will be organ donors. God revealed to me the greatest love of a mother, the mother that gave Taylor a second chance. She doesn't realize that she gave ALL of us life by allowing us to be with Taylor longer than we would have been able to.

I never would have thought to be an organ donor, but I realize now that it is God's way of saying "it isn't your time yet." While you may be experiencing His difficult lesson, for whatever reason, life goes on. So, obviously, there is a purpose. It is just up to the individual to figure out what that might be.

Bambi Cunningham

It's All Gravy

As a young adult, figuring out where my place in the world was, I felt that I was in partnership with God, although I didn't think of that every day or express it verbally. I sort of took it for granted. From past experiences, and with pure trust, I knew God was there and that He was watching over me. He was with me through all of my experiences, through divorce, boyfriends, getting an education, and getting a career going. As a matter-of-fact, it was all His plan.

Time also has allowed me more perspective into what I believe and what God wants, and I can now look back and see God's footprints on my walk. I thought I had arrived, found my religion, and become one of the Christian people I always wanted to be. However, God wasn't quite finished yet. In 2005, the picture of health, I woke up with an illness that can kill, an intestinal blockage. I was in the hospital for a week and had to be operated on, without knowing what all of the consequences might be. It was at this time that I prayed for God's will, and let Him know that I was not afraid of dying if that was what He desired. In other words, I gave up all control, because I knew that only God is in control. It was, literally, a "Catch me, God! If you desire, here I come. I know that you'll be waiting," sort of thing.

Well, needless to say, I'm here, and everything went just fine. In the process, I received a new peace and joy. I also had to learn the great lesson of letting others do for me, even though I felt I could do for myself, so that my friends would also benefit from caring for me. God knew that all of this was important to my walk at that very time.

God gives me my marching orders daily, and I take those orders as opportunities to learn, in whatever environment He places me. Our time is truly short, and we must gather in all of those perfect moments, because we can't count our days. Being incredibly grateful for the life I have, and having faith that I will somehow find a way to make the most out of what God intends for me yet to do, I try to live by God's strength and grace. I pray that I'm living to love my God with all of my heart, soul, mind, and strength, and to love my neighbors as myself, which takes daily effort and prayer. I hope to reach to God in all matters of my life, and not just on the bigger things. I also pray daily that God always knows my deep gratitude. I will continue to thank Him for returning my soul, bruised as it might be, to my body every morning, so that I might continue any kingdom work that He desires me to be apart of. I am at peace, for I know that He is in control, and I am here for His glory. I am also blessed to know that I have made a difference to others. God put me in this position, and family, friends, and students have told me so. I am assured that I have lived for a higher purpose. In this world, that knowledge is more valuable than anything else. As I like to say, "It's all gravy." I just sit back, count my blessings, stay in action mode, and let God do the heavy lifting, so that I may be an example of what Christ means when He calls me to be "the light" in a dark world.

Diane Smith

"The Most Amazing Thing Happened"

When asked about when I first accepted Jesus as my Savior, I am never quite sure how to respond. There isn't a time I can remember when I didn't know Him. I am astounded by this. Where there may be no beginning in my recollection, assuredly there are times that I remember His presence and His divine care of me when I was most in need. From small moments in time that I cherish, to overwhelming burdens I ultimately relinquished, Jesus is and has always been my Rock and Savior.

Once as a middle-school child, I attended a Christian summer camp. While there, we were asked to perform a play. I was given the role of Jesus. The Lord's Prayer was my script and a wonderful camp director worked with me for a heartfelt performance. **The most amazing thing happened;** as I sat on that hillside rock, delivering my best rendition of the Lord's Prayer, it became clear to me that Jesus was sitting right beside me. *Me...a little kid.* Jesus was there, telling me how much He loved me and how He would walk with me throughout the performance. Even now, more than 50 years later, I remember just how close He was. It was the first time I can remember Jesus walking emotionally with me, with the divine gift of love that only He can offer.

After I married, Jesus and I walked together through another difficult time. For five years, my prayer was to be a mother. Patiently, He waited for me to surrender to His will. Finally, I gave it to the Lord in prayer: "Lord, You are in control of my life, and if Your will is for me to be childless, I will be the best I can be. You know my heart is to be a mother, but I want to be pleasing to You, so I lay this burden at Your feet." Once I surrendered, I felt a physical release of my burden. Truly, I felt the comfort and peace that only Jesus can give. In three weeks, **the most amazing thing happened**. We received a call saying that a baby boy had been born and was to be ours by adoption. And then, as if I had only blinked once, eight months passed; I was pregnant with our daughter. Our family was divinely designed in the order God wanted it to be. Surrendering to the Lord should be a simple thing. Why do we make it so difficult, when the rewards are so great?

It was a busy day; my calendar was tightly scheduled with appointments and meetings. Hurriedly, I walked briskly out of my office. "I will be back in an hour or so", I told the receptionist. Through the parking lot, I moved while fishing in my purse for my keys. I spotted my Honda Accord, got in and drove out of the garage into the sunshine and heat of this not-so-typical South Texas afternoon. At this point, everything slowed. I saw a pickup truck turning onto the street I was traveling and the truck was moving closer toward me, pulling a large trailer. However, the trailer was moving at a different tack than the truck. They had separated, the truck and its payload. The truck passed my car on my left and the trailer, carrying a 28-foot, forged steel and metal barbecue pit, was heading straight into my car. Over the hood and through my windshield, slightly under the rear-view mirror, the tongue of this massive trailer came into my car and it extended through the rear window. Inches from my head, the metal bar rested. My ears were ringing and still it seemed to be all in slow motion. Then, **the most amazing thing happened.** "Wilma, you will be okay. It is not your time," she said. How nice, I thought. Someone to wait with me until the police arrive. Shortly, as I looked around for this person, she was no longer there. I then understood that the woman who came to me seconds after the impact was not a passerby, but an angel sent to calm me and care for me. The police stated there was no one there when they arrived. Confirming, *"For He will command His angles concerning you to guard you in all your ways; they will lift you up in their hands, so that you will not strike your foot against a stone."* Psalms 91:11-12. Being in the presence of a Heavenly angel was so inspiring, and yet very humbling. I know that I did not deserve it, but I was very thankful that Jesus gave me His grace and mercy that day, in abundance.

My To-Do List read, "Schedule a mammogram." It had been only ten months since my last one. So, I made the call, had the mammogram and the ultrasound like so many times before. This time, the results were different... breast cancer. Over the next nine months, there were a series of five surgeries at MD Anderson Hospital. It was a life-changing experience. I am a confirmed Type-A personality and find myself often in leadership roles, or at the very least, attempting to be in charge! Not this time. Caught in the flurry of fearing for my life, doctor appointments, trips to Houston, working and managing a fast-paced business, family obligations, surgeries, surgeries and more surgeries, I realized I had no control. Furthermore, I didn't *want* to be in control. Nighttimes were the hardest. I would awake fearfully. And then **the most amazing thing happened.** I, again, surrendered. I learned to lean on Jesus. I would get up out of bed, gather my Bible and go to my special chair. I would rock back and forth and read. He would speak to me thru His word, and calm my fears. Remember the words from the hymn that talks about how He walks with you and talks with you and tells you are His own? He did just that. Those late night moments, with just Jesus and me, were the most precious moments of my life. God *carried* me thru this experience, for I could not walk alone.

Recently, I had the opportunity to parasail. It was a stormy day, with skies that looked like they were painted a dark marbleized blue. The high winds and rough waters would have deterred many novices, but for some strange reason this seemed to be the right time for me. The beauty of the parachute, colored with only the richest and most vibrant colors, took my breath away. And then the winds captured the chute and up I went! **The most amazing thing happened** as the chute carried me higher and higher – there was silence. No wind noise, no rough sea noises, just Jesus and me. It was one of those times God winks for me, reminding me of the magnificence of my Lord and how He tells me how much He loves me at the most amazing times!

Surrendering control has never been easy for me. Certainly, I am a work in progress. Through adversity, and God's unrelenting love, I have learned that even though I am only a speck in God's universe, He is there for me always, especially when I surrender my fears to Him. His glory covers me and His love is my soft pillow to lay my head. **God is always amazing**. Daily, I am thankful to know more of Him.

Wilma Grupe

I Have Put My Trust in You

This is my story describing how Jesus became my best friend.

My parents were Christians, and we were regulars at church. One summer at Vacation Bible School, teachers told stories about Jesus and how He wanted to be our friend forever. All we had to do was ask Him to forgive our sins and believe He would. (Romans 10:9-10)

My parents wanted to be sure that as a 5-year-old, I really understood and was consciously choosing to 'LOVE JESUS WITH ALL MY HEART, SOUL, AND MIND'. We spent some time talking about it, but I was convinced it was the right decision. My mom and our pastor's wife led me in prayer as I asked Jesus to be my Savior and friend on June 7, 1968. (Revelations 3:20). How much do you remember from when you were five? I remember vividly where I was, and the peace that was washing over me.

I was baptized at the age of seven to tell the world I belonged to Him. As an adult, I'm asked how I know that what happened was real. 'Do you really believe

Jesus lives in your heart and is your best friend?' I tell them I experience Jesus every day of my life. He gives me peace, direction, and purpose. Psalms 143:8 is a verse I cling to whether life is sunny or rainy - *'Let the morning bring me word of Your unfailing love, for I have put my trust in You. Show me the way I should go, for to You I lift up my soul.'*

As an adult, I'm sure you've had people let you down. There's no person, no matter how much they love you, who hasn't let you down from time to time. Jesus ALWAYS loves and cares for you. He is the source of love, joy, and happiness. Even when others hurt you, He is there to love, listen, comfort, and provide direction.

My father died on May 7, 2008. He had Alzheimer's, but he never forgot his story of salvation. He was always ready to share it, even when he stumbled with words. For the past three years, I've watched my father walk into the loving arms of Jesus.

When you die, will you find yourself in the loving arms of Jesus, or someplace else, where love does not exist? I can't imagine living forever in a place where there is no love.

Ask Jesus to forgive you, love you, and be with you forever.

God Bless and Keep You,

Liz Patterson

God is in Control

It all began on a beautiful spring day. My daughter Alex was enjoying her spring break with her friends at the beach and enjoying life to its fullest when in an instant it all changed for her and our family.

I am a realtor, so that same day I was on my way to the island on a listing appointment. Well, like all spring breaks (and I should have known better), due to the amount of traffic backed up on the causeway I knew it was going to take quite a bit of time to get there. So I called my client and told him about the traffic and we rescheduled for later that evening. I turned my car around and headed back to town. As I was driving the causeway, I saw Halo Flight flying towards the island. As any mother would, I picked up my cell phone to call Alex just to check on her. Her voice mail came on and I said,"Alex, this is Mom; I just saw Halo Flight heading towards the island and I'm just checking on you. Give me a call." I really did not give it too much thought at the time, and knew Alex would be calling in soon. She was always good about calling me back. Well, I no sooner got back to my office and at my desk than my phone rang. It was one of Alex's friends letting me know Alex had been in a car accident and had been Halo Flighted out, but he did not know which hospital she had been taken to. That was the phone call all parents dread. My first thought was, "Oh my God! I saw the Halo Flight and it was for <u>my daughter</u>, and I don't know where she has been taken or the extent of her injuries." All I knew was that for her to have been Halo Flighted out, it had to be bad.

I got in my car heading down Staples, and pulled into the Wal-mart parking lot. I called Memorial and asked if Alex had been taken there; they put me on hold for what seemed like eternity. When the nurse came back on the phone she said Alex was there, but she could not give me any information, and she told me I needed to come to the hospital. My first thought was that she was dead and they would not tell me on the phone. Frantic, I tried to call my older daughter Shellie and as usual, she did not answer her cell phone. I had kidded her frequently about screening my calls. At a stop light I looked over to my right, and there she was next to me on the phone with her husband, who was telling Shellie where Alex had been taken. She motioned to me to go to Driscoll. WHAT A GOD THING!

But I told her I was told she was at Memorial, so I told Shellie to go to Driscoll and I would go to Memorial. Without realizing it, I found myself in the Driscoll parking lot, not knowing how I got there when I was going to Memorial. Well as it turned out,

Driscoll Children's Hospital is where she had been taken. ANOTHER GOD THING!

To go back to the accident, Alex and her friend Matt had decided to go to the store to get some drinks and snacks. Matt was in the driver's seat and Alex was the passenger. They were in an open Jeep without a top. As always, Alex put on her seat belt. They were driving off of the beach on Zahn Rd and onto 361. As they pulled out, they were T-boned by a drunk driver hitting them at full speed, about 50 miles per hour. Upon impact the jeep flipped over, and for some freak reason Alex's seat belt came unbuckled which caused her to come out of her seat. But instead of being thrown from the Jeep, she was dragged several feet down the highway.

When the paramedics were finally able to get to the scene and assess their injuries, I found out several weeks later that they had pronounced our beautiful Alex dead. They said in the position she was in, and the Jeep was on top of her, there was no way she could be alive. One of the paramedics who saw Alex said "something was tugging at him to go back and check her one more time." ANOTHER GOD THING!

When he went back, knelt down to her, and saw her foot move. Immediately the paramedics threw the Jeep off of her. They called Halo Flight. She barely had a pulse and her blood pressure was almost non-existent. Some how they were able to revive her, and she began talking. They asked her age, she said 15. ANOTHER GOD THING! (Had she said she was 16, she would have been taken to Memorial Hospital instead of Driscoll, where the family was allowed

24-hour access to her. We would not have been able to spend that kind of time with her at Memorial, nor would she have gotten the awesome care she received.). Because she barely had a pulse, and her blood pressure was way below the danger level, Halo Flight asked permission to fly over the naval base and it was granted (which is unheard of). By being able to fly over the naval base, they were able to save a lot of time. Because time was of the essence, the pilot got Alex to Driscoll Hospital in the record-breaking time of four minutes. ANOTHER GOD THING!

When I walked into the emergency room of Driscoll Hospital I was immediately taken into the room where Alex was. The room was full of doctors and nurses working on her. Here is where a little humor comes in, in the middle of all this. You have to know Alex and her strong personality to appreciate it. Here is this child critically injured, and all she was worried about was the nurses cutting off the swimsuit her daddy had just bought her. She was one angry kid. But looking back now, I believe the tough spirit God gave her is what kept her from dying that day.

Well, the story doesn't end here. Alex spent the next eight hours in surgery. Turned out she had multiple internal injuries, head injuries and broken bones. Because she had been dragged down the highway, her whole backside from head to toe and been scraped off. She was the same as a burn victim would be. The doctor was very optimistic she would be okay, but it would take some time. Her biggest fear was being able to fight infection. But other than that,

Alex would be good as new. You can just imagine
our joy and relief. All during this time, the waiting
room stayed full of our friends, family, and even
strangers giving us their love and prayers. Without
them we would not have been able to endure all of
this. Alex spent the next two weeks in intensive care.
Finally she was upgraded to be able to be moved to
a private room. We knew it would just be a matter of
days before we could take her home when our biggest
fear became a reality. On the third day after leaving
intensive care, a deadly infection started taking over
Alex's body. She was rushed back into surgery.
The doctor told us she would need to be intubated,
because in order to take control of the infection she
would need to go to surgery twice a day to debride
her wounds.

On the second evening, I was sitting with Alex
when her doctor came in and did some tests. She told
me Alex's kidneys were starting to fail.

She just was not getting better. "How much more
can this child take?" I asked myself. I went back to
the waiting room where all our friends and family
had been with us from day one. For the first time
I broke down. I knew my little girl was not going
to make it through this one. I was sitting on a chair
when all of a sudden I heard a very loud voice in my
head say, "GIVE HER TO ME." At that moment, I
realized although we have had hundreds of people
praying for her, I had not prayed for her. In my mind,
I felt as long as I didn't pray for God's will for her, I
could hold on to her and God wouldn't take her. But
at that moment, when I heard God's voice, an instant

calm and peace came over me. I knew at that time, if I wanted God to heal my daughter, I was going to have to give her to Him. I went to the chapel, knelt down on my knees and I totally and completely gave Alex to Him. No matter what His plan was, I knew it would be okay. I had total peace. I went back to the waiting room, and my daughter Shellie came running up to me and said, "Mom, the doctor just came back in; they re-ran the test, and Alex's kidneys are okay, they are not failing." From that evening on, Alex began to improve more and more each day. After three months in the hospital, we were able to bring her home. Today she is a 22-year-old young woman working as a Phlebotomist with the Blood Bank. This is one way she is able to give back what was given to her. She hopes to go in the nursing field one day.

As humans, we tend to want to take control of things, and think we can make everything all right. But as Christians, we must always have faith and trust in God, knowing whatever we are going through, He is there carrying us all the way.

I end this with my prayers for you and your family. I hope this will give you hope and encouragement. GOD IS IN CONTROL!

God Bless You Always

Julie Hominick &
Family of Alexandra Hominick

Second Blessing

I am writing to you to let you know of the amazing Grace God has shown our family twice and how my mother and I are so blessed to know firsthand the peace of God's will when you accept it; whether or not it is something you want.

As you have already read or will read in the other testimonies, my sister Alexandra was in a horrible car accident March 2003. I will not retell that story as my mother already has, but what I would like to share with you is my own testimony about my son Colton, which happened July 5, 2009.

We were in Leakey, Texas. We had just picked up our son Colton Trefflich, who is 15, from Laity Lodge Youth Camp on Saturday July 4, and the morning of the 5th we dropped off our daughters, Audrey, 11, and Kylie, 8. Around 5:30 pm my husband, Colton, six of his friends and I went to Garner State Park to relax in the Frio river and enjoy the late afternoon sun. The boys were jumping from the trees and swinging from a rope swing that had been tied from one of the big Cypress trees. Well, my son, much like his Aunt

Alex, has a fearless personality, and a very hard head. Colton has been a daredevil since he could walk. I can remember when he was just able to stand on his own, and he would climb up on our coffee table and throw himself onto the couch. I knew at a very early age I had my hands full with this one.

Anyway, in true Colton fashion, he had to climb a little higher than everyone else on the rope swing. As he was climbing, I was telling him he was too high, and saying to his friends that he always had to outdo everyone, and that one day he was going to get hurt...and no sooner did those words come out of my mouth, than Colton jumped. When he jumped, there was too much slack in the rope, so when the rope became tight it slingshot-ed him to the ground. Yes, the ground, not the water. He landed in the Cypress tree roots and rock. His body slammed to the ground with such force that we could hear his head slam and then watched him slide, lifeless, into the water. Colton's best friend Cooper was there and Colton landed at his feet. As soon as Colton was in the water, he started going under. Cooper jumped in and pulled him out. My husband swam to our son's side, and we were more than sure that he was dead. There was no earthly way a body could endure that kind of fall and live through it without severe injuries or loss of life itself.

I, of course, totally lost it and was screaming, "He's dead, he's dead!" I swam to be by his side and was yelling at him to cling to Christ and to not leave me. My thoughts then turned to prayer. I had to get prayers going, and lots of them. I swam back to shore where I was met by complete strangers ready with open arms to do whatever they could to help. I asked for a phone and was screaming, "Pray... pray, everyone please pray...!" They got a chair for me because at this point I could not stand. All of a sudden I felt this little hand on my shoulder, and could hear the sweetest prayers I have ever heard. Then all the memories of my baby sister's accident started coming back to me. And my thoughts turned to "We used all of our "get out of jail free" passes on my sister; God does not bless a family twice like this." I told the woman who was praying that I could hear God telling me, "It's okay, he's with Me," but as any mother would respond, I did not want MY son with God, I wanted him with me. So I was refusing to hear it, and was refusing the peace that came with it. Then my thoughts turned to..."Oh My Gosh...how amazing are you, God, that at the moment of impact for Colton you were giving me peace, and I knew or thought I knew at that moment my son was in fact dead, and You would get me through it, that my son was with his heavenly Father, my brother in Christ was at home."

But....in that very moment, my husband gave me the thumbs up that Colton had a pulse and a heart beat. As you can imagine, I was beside myself with joy, and it was then that I knew God was with him and healing him before our eyes. All of this and all of these thoughts happened in a matter of moments... maybe 20 minutes or so. Then from that point it has been all up hill. Like my sister, he was airlifted to University Hospital in San Antonio where we spent

24 hours in PICU to keep a watch on him and his head injury. He did have a severe concussion, but that is it. His injury was serious and would require about a 6-month recovery, but to look at him you would never even know he had been through anything.

It is amazing to me that both my mother and I have had to experience the trauma of letting our children go into the hands of God no matter the outcome....and for some reason we were able to keep our children here with us. I guess God had bigger plans for them, or for us. But with that said, I encourage you to cling to Christ anyway you can, and when it is too hard for you to pray, know that there is an army praying in your place. Seek and find the peace of Christ even when it's a peace you don't want to accept. And most of all, know that He LOVES you and will never turn His back on you, and that His will be done.

I pray with all my might that you will have the same victory story as my mother and I, but should yours go a different way, know that the true victory is yours, and that of our Lord, and that the Grace of God will get us through anything; it is there for the taking.

Shellie Trefflich

Not by Sight

Earlier this year my brother, Ronnie Barry, having been diagnosed with Parkinson's Disease, entered the hospital as a result of being given medication to which he reacted badly. The medication caused respiratory and cardiac arrest. He was placed on a ventilator, had a tracheotomy and a feeding tube inserted, and then developed a hospital-acquired infection. Over the course of 18 weeks he also battled pneumonia, intense and constant muscle spasms, and further widespread infections and seizures along with recurring mental confusion. At times, he was restrained in the bed, unable to communicate due to the trach. During these months he was not given food or water by mouth. It seemed to us that every time his condition improved he was knocked down again with some new problem. I remember thinking that it was as though he was in the surf, finally able to stand, when another big wave would come to knock him down. And yet, amazingly enough, by God's grace, Ronnie handled all of this with courage and grace, and never lost his sense of humor. It had to have been God's sustaining power with him day by day, getting him through this nightmare.

One day as I looked at Ronnie in the hospital bed I was overwhelmed with his helplessness, tied to the bed, unable to speak. Then the temptation came to doubt God's care for him. After all, Jesus is the Good Shepherd who protects and cares for His sheep. I remember the thoughts that came to me so clearly. Where is God's care? Where's the Shepherd looking after His sheep? Isn't He supposed to protect us? Where's His care for Ronnie in all this? I cried to the Lord, "I can't see Your care!" Almost immediately, He answered me. "You're looking with human eyes from a human perspective. I'm caring for Ronnie on a level you can't see or even imagine." At that moment I was filled with peace and a deeper trust in God. His assurance of His care for Ron was all I needed. What peace and gratitude I felt as I trusted Him!

I really understand now what Paul meant in 2 Corinthians 5:7. *"We live by faith, not by sight."* My sight was telling me there was no care for Ronnie, but by faith I knew otherwise.

I've come to realize that what we observe in the physical world is only partial reality. The true reality is what God is doing in the spiritual realm. 1 Corinthians 13:12 says, *"Now we see but a poor reflection as in a mirror; then we shall see face to face. Now I know in part; then I shall know fully..."*

So while we, his family and friends, continue to live by faith, Ronnie is no longer living by faith but by sight. He went home to be with his Savior and Good Shepherd on June 10, 2009.

Shirley Evans

In Him,
Shirley Evans

Eric Columbus Edwards
1909-1981

He never sang a solo, but from my earliest memory he was always in his place, third from the left, back row of the choir. He never got up and stirred the congregation with his testimony, but he lived his life in such a way that almost everyone knew his faith in his Lord. He never bought an organ, hung a new bell, or paid for a pew during remodeling. He did, however, give his share faithfully each payday without fanfare.

He lived his life straight up. From the time I first knew he never drank, swore, or used tobacco. Most of his faults could be traced back to what he learned about his fellow man growing up in the Deep South in the twenties.

He worked hard at a carbon black plant, eight and a half hours a day and all the overtime they would give him. He would come home, eat his supper, watch the news, then go to work on some project until ten. He took off Sundays for church, Wednesday night for choir practice, and Saturday afternoon to do any shopping that was needed. I never did figure out what he did in his spare time.

He married one woman and stayed married to her for forty-four years. He loved his Lord, his wife, his family, his country, music, and flying.

He lived his life quietly; He started each day around six with a good-bye kiss and ended each day around ten on his knees thanking his Lord for the blessing given and asking for the forgiveness of his sins.

I don't know for sure, but I suspect, he entered heaven the same way he lived his life on earth, humbly, straight up, seeking his Lord, looking for a choir to sing His praise, and a place to go to work.

Bill Edwards

The Burglar Pilgrim

By practicing a routine of daily prayer and study, I have come to realize some of God's will for my life, yet I could not have known the surprise the Lord had prepared for my husband Dick and me and how deeply it would impact our lives.

One fateful January, a few years ago, our house was burglarized; irreplaceable family heirlooms and valuable personal items were taken. I felt violated, angry and resentful. Both my husband and I wanted justice and were very pleased when the burglars were apprehended. One was our neighbor's daughter, the other her boyfriend; the valuables had been sold for cash to support their drug habit. The scenario could not have been worse.

My initial prayers were for justice; I wanted justice and I wanted it right away. Instead, God placed in my heart the need to pray for these young people. Romans 8:28 became my source of comfort: "*And we know that in all things God works for the good of those who love him who have been called according to His purpose.*" Like an athlete in training, the longer

I practiced praying for "my enemies" the easier it became. I offered daily prayers for these confused and lost souls.

One Saturday afternoon we received a phone call from the father of the young man who had burglarized our house. The father explained that he was in town for 24 hours; his wife and son were in the car with him and he asked if they could stop for a visit. We agreed. Our initial contact was awkward, but something special started to unfold. The young man had been through detoxification at a local hospital and was living in a halfway house undergoing treatment. He wanted to apologize and offered to do some kind of restitution; he asked if he could cut our grass for *the rest of his life*... My husband wished him a long life.

I continued to pray for these two people who had entered my life in such a fateful manner. As the young man worked on our flowerbeds I took the opportunity to visit with him, and as I got to know him a miracle happened. The resentment turned into fondness and the anger started to dissipate. It is hard to hate someone who is loved by God and whom He has placed in my path for me to be a witness.

As the months went by and time came for arraignment, this young man asked us if we would consider dropping the charges – he was facing from 2 to 4 years in prison. My husband was not willing to let him off the hook so easily; in turn he offered him a trade, prison time for a weekend on the Journey to Damascus (a three-day spiritual retreat). The young man agreed; we dropped the charges and immediately signed him up for the next men's Journey. At this point I am excited and thinking, "God, you are so cool." I could see God's hand weaving a soft and tender web to rescue this young man from the forces of evil. We continued to surround him in prayer; we now had a renewed enthusiasm as we could see the possibilities ahead. By now I knew with all my heart that this was a "God thing." Our burglar had become our Pilgrim.

The story could have ended here, but there is more. The weekend of the Journey, my husband and I drove to Laredo to pick up my mother, who was flying in from Mexico City. She was to arrive at noon, so we planned to be back in Corpus Christi in time to join a group of people praying for the pilgrims. As we approached Laredo my cellular phone rang; my mother missed her flight and would not arrive until the evening. All our plans for the day crumbled. We resigned to miss the prayer vigil.

That evening on our way back to Corpus Christi, I realized that the prayer meeting was in process and I decided to join them from the distance. I lifted the pilgrims and my special pilgrim to the Lord, I prayed with all my heart for this young man to be delivered from the stronghold of evil and the demons of drugs. I prayed to the Omnipotent God, the One who can move mountains if needed, and I claimed this young man for Him. At that moment all the lights in the car went out. We were moving at 65 miles an hour on a dark and busy highway with no headlights. My husband managed to stop and proceeded to manipulate light switches to no avail.

At this point I returned to my prayer with a renewed conviction and energy. I felt that the forces of good and evil were at play and in blind faith, with all my might, I continued to reclaim for God the soul of our Pilgrim. In all honesty I did not have an understanding of what was happening; I just had faith. Suddenly, the car lights came back on, and the car engine, which had been heating up, cooled down and we were able to continue our trip. The rest of our journey was without incident. I don't know if our car trouble was in any way related to a supernatural event, what I do know is that something amazing happened that night at the retreat center.

As we picked up our pilgrim on Sunday, he shared with us that the night before, about the time of our troubles and prayers, he had felt compelled to stand up and share his story with the rest of the pilgrims. His act of contrition moved the group to a standing ovation. He expressed his experience as if a heavy weight had been lifted off his shoulders.

I pray that this young man turns his life around for good. There is no doubt in my mind that God is working on him even now. I also know that God had a much more meaningful lesson for Dick and me. Forgiveness did more for us than for our young friend. Our resentment and anger disappeared and love took their place. I feel love for this young man. What he took from our home does not compare with what God gave us in return.

Bea Hanson

The Lord's Leading

I was baptized when I was twelve, to please my mother. When I was twenty, I quit college after two years because I didn't know what I wanted to major in; Teaching or nursing were the two main fields open to women at that time, and I wasn't interested in either. I tried building a goat dairy, but I was no businesswoman. About that time I remember standing under a cork elm tree outside our kitchen and telling the Lord, "I'm making a mess of things. Now I'm ready to do it Your way."

Not long after that I was asked to substitute teach older children in Sunday School and to lead a Girl Scout troop. I wasn't yet twenty-one.

I forsook the goats and got a job in the Dean's Office of the University of Louisville School of Medicine. During the time I was there I met and married my husband, and we had our first son. By the time our second son started kindergarten I told my husband, "I'm bored. I either want to get a job or start back to school." He said, "I'd rather you went back to school." I started out with just one course but kept increasing the load. When I was a senior, my school was trying to get Southern accreditation, and required that all graduating seniors take the National Teacher's Exam and the Graduate Record Exam. It cost us nothing but time and effort. After I graduated, my husband said, "Now that you can teach I want to quit my job." Then when my husband died suddenly of a heart attack, I decided to teach full time, and since I would now be the breadwinner, go back to school and get my master's degree.

I was the one who hadn't wanted to be a teacher but once I quit fighting, the Lord led me into that occupation. I retired after many years as an elementary school counselor.

The Lord has guided me all along the way once I decided to let Him.

Elma D. Holden

God Is Great

In Mass one evening, on a recent Journey to Damascus spiritual retreat, a priest spoke of faith. It hit me how even though I'd never turned away from God or doubted His Holy Being, I went through a period when I lost faith that God would see me through the mess my life had become.

Many years ago, I felt as though my life was hopeless. I had found myself recently divorced, laid off from the company I'd worked for over 16 years, and, at the same time, was diagnosed with a possibly fatal disease.

Prior to losing my health insurance, I began a treatment program that causes people to become quite despondent even under the best circumstances. Sapped of my strength from the powerful meds I was on, I spent a lot of time in bed and was unable to obtain work. I'd lost a good deal of my hair and a lot of weight. I could have handled the illness; however, without the income I had depended on, my life was in ruins.

My daughter was still living at home and attending college. And, she was still my number one responsibility. Not a day went by that I didn't cry over how I would pay my bills. I labored over where I'd find the money to keep the utilities turned on, make the car payments, pay my mortgage, and a multitude of other debts.

How could this happen to me? Why was it happening to me? How was I to live? I was totally hopeless with nowhere to go and no one to bail me out. I was not able to make decisions wisely as my depression and meds had put me in a very dark place.

I cried everyday and desperation consumed my being, as I went through the loss of all my worldly possessions - my savings, my home, my car, everything! If not for my Christian faith and knowing that I had a family that loved me, it could have all ended.

My health insurance ran out before my treatment ended; however, our gracious Lord saw that I was healed. While trying to regain my strength my family provided me with a home to live in and helped me with my debt. My daughter had become engaged and found a new home with her husband.

It has taken many years to get back on my feet. However, I am now employed and my story has become a happy one. I was fortunate; as God lived in my family home while I was growing up, I had been taught of His eternal love and salvation.

I'm a survivor of the disease and misery that crippled me for years. God spared my life. And, yes, I've found love again. He led me to the love of my life and I'm very happily married. My husband is an awesome man of God. My daughter is doing well, and is happy with children of her own. I am so blessed!

He lives, and He lives within me. I pray I never lose faith again. There's nothing fair about the things that happen to us in this life, but with God all things are possible. We know not the hour nor the day that God will take us to our heavenly home or what twists and turns lie ahead. There's nothing easy about life, but we can't lose our faith.

These have come so that your faith—of greater worth than gold, which perishes even though refined by fire—may be proved genuine and may result in praise, glory and honor when Jesus Christ is revealed. 1 Peter 1:7

Ashley J.

Leave It in God's Hands

What began as a horrible accident with a drunk driver, God used to save my life. Early one morning, I was traveling on the highway with a friend. A truck coming the other way suddenly pulled right out in front of me. Having seconds to react, I slammed on the brakes, hit the horn, and pulled my steering wheel as hard as I could. I almost made it, when he darted in front of me again. When we collided, I saw pieces of my car slowly float in the air, and as my car rose, I went unconscious. When I woke up, someone was yanking on my door. My friend yelled that the police were on their way. The other driver jumped back in his truck and attempted to flee. I prayed for God to stop him. He turned into a pasture and attempted to cross the railroad tracks, getting his truck wedged tight. He tried pushing and jumping on the back end while his girlfriend gunned the engine to no avail. My husband said it was God saying, "Thou shall not leave the scene of the accident." When this didn't work, he walked over and stood near my car just staring at us. (I prayed for the

Lord to protect us.) He pulled a lighter out of his pocket and tried to light it, but it just wouldn't ignite. When a fireman appeared and tackled him saying, "You could blow them up, can't you smell the gas!" I found out later that the guy I was in a wreck with has been in and out of prison with a long rap sheet. Our Lord will protect us in our hour of need.

I was transported to the hospital and released. When I still wasn't okay after a couple of days I went to the doctor. He said I had a concussion and whiplash, but after several weeks of treatment I still wasn't doing well. I was sent to a neurologist. After several tests they found out I had a basilar tip aneurysm that required immediate surgery. I was sent to Houston, and that doctor explained that once I felt the symptoms of a rupture I would be dead within minutes. I didn't have insurance and began to fall into despair. Then the Lord lifted me up, speaking words of encouragement. He asked, "Do you trust me?" I said, "Of course, with my life." He said, "Then leave it in my hands and all will be taken care of. For what you cannot do I can, but you can not take it back. You have to leave it to Me." I said, "For Your honor, glory, and praise, I trust that there is no bad outcome. Even in death I am with You, but my concern is for my family." He whispered, "Have faith, and trust in Me." Instantly he flooded me with His peace and love. What our Lord did for me surpassed anything I could possibly imagine! Several fund raisers sprang up, raising money from all over. It was all happening so fast, and anytime I tried to get involved, everything would fall apart until I gave it back to Him.

A TV station did an interview, and a friend I hadn't seen in a while arrived at my doorstep to hand me a substantial check. People who I didn't know were giving from their hearts and many from their wallets. I was being truly blessed. Before long we had enough to schedule the surgery.

Unfortunately things did not go well in surgery. The artery in my left leg ruptured and they needed to halt the surgery. The surgeon felt God intervened, because my aneurysm had grown dramatically and this gave them time to come up with a plan. I remained in the ICU, and was taken down for another surgery the next day. They thought all had gone well, but they could not wake me up. They rushed me for a CT scan and found that I had hemorrhaged. I was rushed to surgery to have a shunt put in my brain to alleviate the pressure and remove the blood. The prognosis was bleak. They braced my family, telling them I could remain in a coma, and if I were to come out of it the damage might be extensive. By God's hand I woke up. Then things took a turn for worse; I had a minor stroke and began running a temperature of 104°. For the next week and a half they battled to keep my temperature down by putting me on a 32° ice bed. When that failed to work, they ran iced saline solution through my veins at 3 points.

My blood pressure kept plummeting. I was at the end of any strength I could muster; I just couldn't do it any more. I had collapsed, my heart was erratic, my temperature was on the rise, and machines were wailing, signaling my body's distress. Although many people rushed into my room, there wasn't anything they could do. I was in God's hands. I cried out for God to help, I just couldn't do this. One of my nurses stepped forward and sat beside me on the bed and began to pray with many others. Immediately, I received the strength I needed, and my heart regained a normal rhythm. A complete sense of peace washed over the room. That was the last day I had any temperature, and I dramatically improved. The day after that they began to teach me how to walk again. Three days later, I was toddling without the use of a walker. I was released from the ICU and 24 hours later was released from the hospital. The doctors were astounded. Several commented that God was truly watching over me. With all I have been through the doctors only gave me a 2% chance of survival. Miraculously, after all that had occurred, I had very little damage. They still call me the miracle patient. I thank God every day for what he has done for me, and for putting such caring people in my life.

I still have problems, but the Lord continues to lift me up with encouragement. Our great Lord and Savior, Jesus Christ, continues to surpass all human understanding. He has given me a greater under-standing of Proverbs 3:5-6 *"Trust in the Lord with all your heart and lean not on your own understanding, in all your ways acknowledge Him and He will make your paths straight."*

Cheryl Johnson

Child of God

"If you remain in me, and my words remain in you, ask whatever you wish, and it will be given you." John 15:7

"He set his seal of ownership on us, and put his Spirit in our hearts as a deposit, guaranteeing what is to come." 2 Corinthians 1:22

I was two when Mom and Dad divorced. My mother's parents helped raise me, and let me say, they had 17 children of their own! There were four boys still at home when I went to live with them.

Picture in your mind a three-story farm house that sat in the middle of 200 acres in Southern Illinois. So you can only imagine the "chores to be done" (that's what Grandfather called them). My Grandmother was about 4'9", always had an apron on when cooking, which was most of the time, and a bonnet when she was in the vegetable or flower garden. They grew everything we ate, canned the vegetables and fruit, and Grandmother's jams and jellies would put any of the name brands to shame!

The day started at 4:00 AM. You see, Grandmother cooked on a wood-burning stove, and every morning she made homemade biscuits, and cooked bacon, ham, sausage, eggs, and cream gravy, and of course, served them with jelly, jam, and honey. At 4:30 AM, Grandfather would call to the boys on the 3rd floor, and if he did not hear them hit the floor, he would start up the stairs with razor strap in hand. And believe me, when they heard him coming, you would hear all of them hit the floor because before they left for school, the hogs had to be fed, the cows milked and fed, as well as the other farm animals fed.

One of my chores was to help gather the eggs, and on Saturday we would take the eggs in an egg basket to the store. The store owner would ask how many dozen we had and would never question us when we told him the amount. He would say, "Mrs. Dawson, get what you need", and of course, all she ever needed was coffee, sugar, and flour. She would always say, "Child (that was me because she couldn't remember my name!), come with me", and we would go to the back of the store and pick out the sacks of flour and sugar. The material the sacks were made of was very pretty and good quality, and two sacks would make me a dress so we had to find two just alike, and Grandmother let me pick my favorite. One of my other jobs was to churn the milk to make the butter and then put the butter in the molds.

Holidays were very special, especially Christmas. Grandfather would cut the Christmas tree, always the biggest one! We decorated with popcorn and cranberry strings and homemade decorations made by all the grandchildren. Grandfather was always Santa Claus, and Grandmother made sure we all had gifts under the tree, especially the grandchildren. "Santa Claus", Grandfather, would have a little brown sack with oranges, nuts, and peppermint sticks to give to each of the small children. Remember, there were 17 children in the family so when they brought their families, there were 60 to 70 of us! A good time was had by all! We sang Christmas carols and talked about what Christmas was really all about.

On Sunday mornings, Grandmother would say, "Child, come let me fix your hair". I always dreaded that because she would heat the curling iron in the kerosene lamp, and it would get so hot you could hear my hair sizzle, but believe me, I had curly hair! Then she would say, "Child, let's go pick the flowers", which we would put on the piano in the little country church we attended. On the way to church, Grandmother would sing "Amazing Grace", "Old Rugged Cross", and "What a Friend We have in Jesus". The church didn't have a choir but they didn't need one because my Grandmother and Aunt would sit on the front pew and sing to the top of their voices, and 9 times out of 10 the preacher would come home with us for dinner.

Grandmother always said to me, "Child, there is good in everyone, you just have to look long and hard for some", and in the family Bible she wrote these words, "Work Hard, Worry Little and Pray Much". What wisdom she had!

So you can see how my walk with Jesus started. Remember, I told you that my Grandmother called me "Child". Many years later I realized how special that name was, because you see, I Am a Child of God, and so are each and every one of you!

June Pearce

We are All God's Children

We are all His children, uniquely created in the image of God, a gift of God, planted where we are to do His work. Each and every person is important in the kingdom of God.

I was born Baby Murphy in Seattle, Washington, October 12, 1948, to God's liking and choosing. I was given up for adoption. Six months later, Reverend and Mrs. Clifton Morgan, returning from their Chaplaincy stint in Tokyo, stopped by and changed my destiny. They adopted me.

When I was the tender age of ten, my parents told me about the opportunity of a lifetime. We had been selected to become the first African American Missionaries for the Church of God which has its headquarters in Anderson, Indiana. What a privilege! What an honor! What an experience!

Upon arriving in India at the age of eleven, I stayed with my parents on the "plains" for six months. The plains are described as a land that is not in the mountains, where I would later attend school.

On the plains, my mother became the Headmistress for the girls' high school and assisted my father with the administration duties of the orphanage that our church called "The Shelter". My parents also assisted with the church ministry and any other duties required in the city of Cuttack, Orissa, about 150 miles southeast of Calcutta. I usually played the pump organ for the church, taught Sunday School, and befriended many of the Shelter Orphanage girls. I became especially close to one named Ruth. Ruth is the biological sister of my Indian sister that my parents took in. (Giti, my Indian sister, now lives in Saint Petersburg, Florida.)

I learned to speak the Oriya, the Indian language of the state of Orissa. I became my parents' translator. After six months of living on the plains with my parents, my parents took me to the private American School that I would be attending for the next four years. It was a four-day train ride away from my parents, so later I often joked with my parents that I really reared myself (of course that is not true – God did). My parents were placed in another part of Orissa State, called Keonjhar after three years in Cuttack. Keonjhar had never had any westerners, so this was truly an interesting experience.

In 1965 we returned to the United States and resided in Pittsburgh, Pennsylvania for one year. While my parents were going around the country telling about the goodness of God and the missionary work they had been performing, I was finishing my high school work. My parents then traveled to Anderson, Indiana, left me with people I did not know, and returned to India for five more years of missionary work. I was in the United States by myself.

In the interim, I completed my college degree, traveled to California to work on my Masters Degree, and returned to Indiana to be closer to my parents who had now returned from the Missionary field and started working for General Motors Company. In 1975 my oldest daughter, Cesha, developed a heart problem at the age of six months. Because her heart stopped one day while we where at home, I had to rush her, lifeless, to the hospital. Since she was without oxygen for a long period of time, she developed cerebral palsy. (Prior to this experience, she had been normal.) They pronounced that not only would she not live, she definitely would not make it through the night. Praise God that man does not control our destinies. Cesha will turn 34 years old in November, Lord willing.

The Lord watched over me and made all the things in my path successful. In many instances he put me into positions of promotion and protected my career when my job title was being downsized and done away with. At every turn God provided for me and my daughter. I was faithful even when I moved to Laredo, TX without knowing a soul.

The rest is history . . . I have now been blessed with Monay (my thirteen-year-old granddaughter) and Kenneth Robert Schmies, my husband of twelve years, three great stepchildren, and a host of friends who are really like relatives. I attend a wonderful church, serving God with the utmost of my abilities. I have retired from General Motors/Delphi after thirty-six and a half years of service, and am planning to teach at our local community college in a few weeks. I am also working as a consultant for my own company.

God is awesome. When I was born it may have looked like I was alone and had nothing, but to God I am a princess and He took me in, protected me and made my paths straight. He has a design for each of our lives. We just need to follow Him. He will enrich our lives. Praise God for that enrichment. Praise God for His protection and divine intervention on our behalves. He helps us live our very blessed lives.

So may God richly bless you as He has me. May you serve Him with all of your heart and mind. May you come to know Him if you do not now. With God at the center of your life, you cannot fail.

God bless you, Taylor!

Carolyn Schmies

Love Cookies

Normally, when one thinks of baking memories, you remember baking in the kitchen with mom. I have many wonderful memories baking with my mother, but nothing can compare to baking love cookies, because you see, they had the most love in them.

When I was a young girl growing up in Grand Prairie, Texas, I was what you might call a high maintenance child. Since it was in the late nineteen fifties, the labels of being emotionally disturbed or prone to anxiety attacks were not used in connection with children, but I could have easily fit into those categories. It was with these problems that I arrived in the first grade, I had so much self inflicted perfectionism that every time I could not do something perfectly on the first try I would get nauseated, throw up, and have to go home. Needless to say, I missed about half of the first grade and ended up with stomach ulcers. The ulcers made me even more of an odd duck, since there was no cure for them at that time; people thought you had to cure them nutritionally. So every day in second grade I had to march to the lunchroom and drink milk. I also took medication which my mother called my "nerve" pills. I think you now can get the picture of what I meant by high maintenance.

It was during this time of my life that we had some new neighbors move in across the street. They were a friendly family and had two girls about the age of my sister and me. We all became fast friends. I think it was providential that they moved there when they did and that "Miss Golda" had the opportunity to observe me day to day. Knowing her spiritual convictions as well, I'm sure she spent quality time praying for my many needs. The family didn't live across the street from us for very long until they had to move away. Lucky for me, we all remained friends. Wherever they would move we would still get together and all of us would spend days and nights at each other's houses. Because of my many anxieties, it was hard for me to spend the night at other people's houses. Without saying a word though, "Miss Golda" always made me feel at home. Because of my ulcers, my diet was very bland; I had trouble finding food I really liked. This was where the Love Cookies came into being. Miss Golda would always bake these cookies for me every time I came to visit. Those cookies, along with her gentleness, gracious hospitality, and loving care, eased my anxieties and calmed my many fears so I could enjoy myself.

Miss Golda and her two daughters are still friends of mine. We get together a couple of times a year to visit. The fears and anxieties that I had as a child have long disappeared but I have never forgotten the lesson of the Love Cookies. For twenty years I taught elementary school specializing in children with emotional problems. I never forgot the secret of the Love Cookies. I am now sharing that secret with you.

Over my lifetime, I have varied the recipe to accommodate every holiday. I have made iced Christmas cookies, Easter cookies, Valentine's Day cookies, and Thanksgiving cookies.

Love Cookies

2 ½ cups sugar
2 sticks butter
1 tsp. vanilla
3 eggs
Mix well.
4 cups flour
1 tsp. baking powder
½ tsp. soda
Chill dough. Cut out shapes or use a drinking glass to make round cookies. Bake at 350. Sprinkle with cinnamon, ginger, or sugar if desired. Can also be iced.

Oh, yes, I almost forgot. These cookies won't come out right if not baked with love. Do you know a child or adult who needs some tender loving care? Bake and take these cookies out into the world and spread a little sunshine. There could be someone on your block who needs some Love Cookies.

Gwen McMath

Forgiveness is a Gift

I accepted Jesus into my heart at the age of eleven at a small church in Lancaster, TX. Shortly there-after we moved and I never became involved in another church. Left undiscipled and a teenager in the '70s, soon I fell into a group that drank alcohol and smoked marijuana. I became sexually active at the age of 16 and had an abortion at 18. After this I did slow down some and tried to clean up my act and live more responsibly.

In the mid '90s I felt the pressures of life building up for me. In addition to pressures from my job, my biological clock started ticking. After months of infertility treatments and many unanswered prayers, I really began to unravel. I had, at this point gone back to church. I knew I needed help, but it just wasn't showing up. I remember praying to God each and every month for those years. Lord, you know I am a really good person at heart. I've done some bad stuff, and made some bad decisions, but I've learned from that and I really am trying to be a better person. But what was really bugging me is that little voice in my head that kept reminding me that I didn't deserve to have my prayers answered. I kept hearing that voice. What it said was, "YOU'RE NOT WORTHY!"

Then in 1997 I ended up at a Christian retreat. I heard a young woman give her testimony. How tragic her life story was. I began to ponder cynically. "I wonder just what kind of Christian woman is she really?" Has she been able to forgive and forget and really go on with her life? Well just then God spoke to me. He turned that question back at me and said "Have you been able to forgive and forget?" The answer was no. I had suffered at the hand of people to my wits end and of course could not forgive myself for the choices I had made. But the Lord knew I wanted to be forgiven. Oh, I had asked for God to forgive me over and over again. But what! Was He listening? What was it that God wanted of me? Well, He wanted me to be obedient. Matt 6:14. *"For if you forgive men when they sin against you, your heavenly Father will also forgive you."* Okay! So I started this personal inventory of people who I held a grudge for and stopped early in the list.

The next thing I knew I was writing to a man in prison that had killed my deaf/mute brother in 1981. What I explained is that God had finally shown me that I was no different from him. His sin was no greater than mine and I was writing to let him know I had forgiven him and that I had found forgiveness for all the things I did, with the help of Christ Jesus.

I have to admit to you that the original intent of this letter was strictly selfish. I was just being obedient to what God had told me so that I could receive the forgiveness that I so badly needed — but God always has another plan. I did not expect it, but three weeks later I received a letter from Kevin. He explained how he had longed for my letter. Knowing he could never take away any of the pain he had inflicted on my family he wanted me to know he felt remorse. I began to feel the weight of the world lift off of me. Suddenly, I had a joy about me that I had not experienced for some time.

Two years later we corresponded again. The Holy Spirit moving through the words of my first letter touch Kevin and I learned that he had also found his salvation and forgiveness in the Lord. He was sharing our testimony of forgiveness and reconciliation in prison.

In reaching out to God and submitting to him in obedience, I found my life again. But it was the amazing grace of God revealed in forgiveness that helped another find his. I never imagined in my wildest dreams that God would use me, worthless me, to reach out to someone else; that his life would be changed and he would be used to save someone else.

Well, as a result of this I look at myself differently. More importantly, I look at others differently. Most anyone who's not perfect is pretty much just like me. I now look at conflict and turmoil and being at the bottom differently because that's where I can see God work His biggest miracles in my life.

Before, I couldn't see my sin. Like Kevin I looked at everything from my own perception of what was right or wrong. I let the world set the benchmark for how to live my life. I explained away my actions and justified my sin and reconciled myself to the world and the world alone. It was only when I had the guts to admit that the way I saw and did things was sinful in the eyes of God that He took that sin and washed it clean; making me new.

> *"Therefore, if anyone is in Christ he is a new creation, the old has gone and the new has come. All this is from God, who reconciled us to himself through Christ and gave us the ministry of reconciliation. We are therefore Christ's ambassadors, as through God were making his appeal through us. We implore you on Christ's behalf; be reconciled to God."*
> 2 Cor 5:18

I am worthy. God proved that when he sent His son to die on a cross for me. Because I believe, God can use me for furthering His work in the kingdom. Yes, the results of my personal petition set me free, as well as a few other people who were in my path. Thank you, Lord.

Terri Shook

The Goodness of God Gives Life

God granted us the heritage of children to reveal His goodness through the trials and afflictions He called us to bear. It began with our precious baby girl. After hours of unproductive labor, the obstetrician finally tugged with forceps, and out slid Baby into Daddy's cradled arms. Warm bath water trickled across her silky skin as Daddy gently soothed her troubled entrance into this world. Oh how perfect she looked! We instantly bonded with this wailing baby whose head bore a painful hematoma. Fears mounted as the doctor detected a loud heart murmur. By the third day our fears lifted when the pediatrician dismissed her from the hospital with an "innocent" heart murmur. Truly a gift from God—His goodness was upon our family. We traipsed back to the hospital three weeks later for her well-baby check-up with her scrawny body weighing nearly two pounds lighter than birth weight. Doctors whisked her away for heart tests. Surely God's goodness would be with her. Better nursing procedures helped her weight thrive. Two years lapsed with regular cardiology check-ups. Then our robust newborn son sprung on the scene. This bundled blessing found himself in the care of Granddaddy and Grandmother as his sister underwent a heart catheter and angioplasty, opening her severely narrowed pulmonary valve. God was indeed good to us.

As she potty-trained, why the deep reddish brown liquid in the toilet? Another trip to the doctor led to a hospitalization of extensive tests. The dreaded words, "chronic kidney disease," stretched our faith to trust God with a trial that would last eleven years. Hospitals, second opinions, collecting urine samples, blood draws, more tests, treatments, medications, chemotherapy, and suddenly another newborn boy graced our lives. God's precious gift—again—but what about the gift of healing that we pleaded for day and night? Was God good in spite of the bad things happening to us? We delivered baby #3 in a hospital room one floor away from our sweet daughter who nearly drowned in pericardial effusion fluids strewn around her heart.

My heart sank when my husband and I left our two-week-old son behind to take our daughter to a hospital hundreds of miles away in another state. Physicians prescribed a hopeful course of medications and a fluid restriction. Months later we returned to the hospital only to find the treatment had deceived us. "Now we must wait until her kidneys completely fail," said the pediatric nephrologist. "It will only take about eighteen months, and she will regain energy and feel much better once she begins dialysis." Certainly not our princess! Surely the Great Physician cared enough to prevent kidney failure, and He would not force her to live on dialysis. Hadn't she been through enough already? We weren't about to sit around and watch her kidneys fail without a fight. God was good and He would do us good. Yet prayer chains united all over the country did not help arrest the disease. Meaningful cards to comfort and cheer could not soothe her nearly lifeless body. Friends helped us pick up broken pieces of our hearts as our spunky daughter digressed to a lethargic state of sleep nearly 20 hours each day. We knew God was there, but where? We cried out to Him in utter helplessness. He answered our prayers from Himself. *Thou art good, and doest good; teach me thy statutes* (Psalm 119:68).

God visited us through the comfort of the Scriptures and through caring people. No matter how bad things seemed, God was good, and the evil happening to us He meant for our good. Daily uplifting cards appeared in our mailbox from friends or people who did not even know us. Unexpected meals dropped into our kitchen. The Spirit comforted, helped us endure, and gave us faith to believe Him to do what would give Him greatest pleasure. *But our God is in the heavens: He hath done whatsoever He hath pleased* (Psalm 115:3). It was not enough to believe He could or would heal our daughter. It mattered that His goodness would be known and shown. He knew what was best, and He would perform it by His own will, according to His own purpose, and for His own glory.

Sure enough, eighteen months after beginning the kidney treatment, her kidneys failed and she began dialysis. A two-week training class landed us parents the role of dialysis nurse at home with our daughter and her noisy cycler machine. Each night we connected her to the machine. Twenty-minute intervals lapsed before the machine emptied the used fluid and flushed a fresh round of dialysate fluid into her peritoneum. Morning and evening patterns of sterile dressing changes around the catheter site and confinement to a machine eight hours per night became our daughter's "normal" life. God graciously held her alive by His goodness and grace and through dialysis.

Our daughter's health problems did not keep her from asking for a new baby sister. She desired a sister even more than her own healing. Daily she prayed, and by God's goodness, He answered her prayers. At long last she had a living doll girl to whom she would sing, dress, and cradle in her arms. This baby blessing was only five months old when our daughter's dialysis catheter plugged up and she had to return to the hospital for 2 ½ weeks of IVs and another catheter placement surgery.

Five years later another baby boy blessing arrived, bringing great joy to our household. Our daughter continued peritoneal dialysis at home each night as we sported a supposedly better dialysis machine. Soon after beginning its use, however, the machine stalled, forcing contaminated fluids into our daughter, and she contracted fungal peritonitis. Doctors in the hospital treated her for a bacterial infection, waiting for a culture to grow for a proper diagnosis. Our daughter's excruciating pain intensified until we finally learned eight days later that she was being treated with the wrong medication. We spent forty days and forty nights in a hospital wilderness two hundred miles away from our family. Our three-month baby boy stayed nearby with Grandma who brought him to visit us once a week. He was the only source who could put a smile on our daughter's face during this intense trial.

And I said, My strength and my hope is perished from the LORD: Remembering mine affliction and my misery, the wormwood and the gall. My soul hath them still in remembrance, and is humbled in me. This I recall to my mind, therefore have I hope. It is of the LORD's mercies that we are not consumed, because His compassions fail not. They are new every morning: great is Thy faithfulness. The LORD is my portion, saith my soul; therefore will I hope in Him. The LORD is good unto them that wait for Him, to the soul that seeketh Him. It is good that a man should both hope and quietly wait for the salvation of the LORD. It is good for a man that he bear the yoke of his youth. He sitteth alone and keepeth silence, because He hath borne it upon him. He putteth his mouth in the dust; if so be there may be hope. He giveth his cheek to him that smiteth him: he is filled full with reproach. For the LORD will not cast off for ever: But though He cause grief, yet will He have compassion according to the multitude of his mercies. For He doth not afflict willingly nor grieve the children of men. To crush under his feet all the prisoners of the earth. To turn aside the right of a man before the face of the most High, To subvert a man in his cause, the LORD approveth not. Who is he that saith, and it cometh to pass, when the Lord commandeth it not? Out of the mouth of the most High proceedeth not evil and good? Wherefore doth a living man complain, a man for the punishment of his sins? Let us search and try our ways, and turn again to the LORD. Let us lift up our heart with our hands unto God in the heavens (Lamentations 3:18-41). God used this wilderness experience to humble our family and grow us in character and He taught us to know Him, trust His Word, and number our days in this short life.

At long last we were able to return home greeted by clinging squeals and hugs. With two weeks at home, only to be led back to the hospital for another round of surgeries, our daughter cried out with extreme discouragement. "Why does God hate me? Why doesn't He just kill me? Why does He keep torturing me with all these problems and pain?" Three additional months forced a total of six surgeries replacing central lines and adding drain lines to rid her of abscesses and adhesions from the surgeries. God's good hand of providence would lead her through this wilderness into a land of promise.

Six and one half years of peritoneal dialysis at home ended forever when her peritoneal cavity completely scarred down from abscesses and adhesions. We only had hemodialysis to clean her blood.

The harshness of hemo left her feeling sickly. Her catheter quit working which meant another surgery to replace the central line. This occurred several times over the next fourteen months. The only opportunity for extended life was a kidney transplant. She waited on a transplant list and we began praying for God's will—praying for the right kidney with excellent antigen matches. We prayed for the donor and the donor's family. Knowing someone would die and the family would donate the organs, we prayed for their eternal life, that they would come to know Jesus Christ as their savior and Lord. Someone's time on earth was short, and we prayed they would be prepared for the trauma to come and spend good quality time with their family before that day arrived. *Precious in the sight of the LORD is the death of his saints* (Psalm 116:15). Then God called one of His saints home to abide with Him in heaven.

Our call came from the children's hospital in another state. I heard the dialysis nurse say, "Are you ready for some good news? Get to the hospital right away." A child died. An excellent donor. Our daughter was a four out of six antigen match with the donor, and she was next on the list to receive this kidney. Emotions soared with elation for our daughter but plummeted with grief for the family whose precious child died tragically. Ironically, our child's eleven-year kidney disease was replaced by the kidney from an eleven-year-old child. The end of one's healthy life on earth provided the end of sickly health for another. Our daughter thrived with her new kidney. She felt "normal" again. She tasted food again. She energized. Her new kidney enabled new opportunities. Lovely music flowed from her voice. She finished schooling, graduated from nursing school, and worked as an RN, serving others whose health waned. Most of all, she acknowledged that God is good and all His works are done in righteousness. *His work is honourable and glorious: and his righteousness endureth forever* (Psalm 111:3).

One of the good works of God was in saving our kidney donor's life from the eternal destruction of hell. Through unusual circumstances God graciously enabled us to learn that prayers for our donor's salvation had been answered. Neighbor children and their parents befriended and took this child, who would die in a few months, to their church. Before death, the child trusted in Jesus and repented from sin. This was another great cause for rejoicing, and we anticipate meeting in heaven one day.

God is indeed good. We see His goodness in the blackest night seasons and in the brightest days of graciousness. No matter what happens, though all about us changes, He never changes. *For I am the LORD, I change not; therefore ye sons of Jacob are not consumed* (Malachi 3:6). Trials gracing our lives through five blessings of children are worth every weight of affliction in anticipation of God's work and glory in time and eternity. *For our light affliction, which is but for a moment, worketh for us a far more exceeding and eternal weight of glory; While we look not at the things which are seen, but at the things which are not seen: for the things which are seen are temporal; but the things which are not seen are eternal* (2 Corinthians 4:18). The Psalms express our hearts in words. *I would have despaired unless I had believed I would see the goodness of the LORD In the land of the living. Wait for the LORD; Be strong and let your heart take courage; Yes, wait for the LORD* (Psalm 27:13-14). God used every speck of trial to train us to follow the Lord and live by His Word. *It is good for me that I have been afflicted; that I might learn thy statutes* (Psalm 119:71). It is truly worth enduring every painful trial in this fallen world because, *He makes everything beautiful in His time* (Ecclesiastes 3:11a).

Anonymous

Copyright July 2009. All rights reserved. Used by permission.

Are You Afraid?

As far back as I can remember there has been fear in my life story. Fear of abandonment was my first introduction to the sense of uncertainty and insecurity that pursued me through my early years of life. My young mother's marriage didn't last through my second birthday. With a failed marriage, a two-year old, and pregnant again, my mother entered the workplace fulltime to provide financially for her children. My mother's parents, a couple of nannies, and childcare centers became the extended family, filling the void of my parents' absence. I hated being out of visual range of my mother because with my fears I couldn't fully trust that she would come back for us. My father hadn't…maybe one day she wouldn't, either.

Elementary school in the early 60's brought a new fear in the form of something called an air raid drill. Thousands of American school children were taught to respond to the sound of sirens that would cue us to assume a position of safety under our wooden desks. In the event we were attacked by the enemy, we were to hunker down on the floor with one forearm under the head and the other arm over our head, hand cupped over our ears to drown out the noise of the siren and whatever fallout might come from the blast that ended life as we knew it. For a first grader, whether the supposed enemy was Cold War Russia, Communist Cuba or just an A-bomb of unknown origin, it mattered not. We were away from home and families. In my mind we might not go home one day.

I began to carry fear with me everywhere like the weight of a college kid's book-filled backpack strapped to his back. It found me everywhere I ventured. Even spending the night away from home had unknown threats to my peace of mind. The role that my maternal grandparents played in my life was vital to my upbringing and sense of security, but the enemy of fear was even lurking there in the form of death this time. Every weekend visit was overflowing with love and security *until darkness set in*. Then the thoughts of dread and loss would enter my mind. During the wee hours of the night, I would catch myself waking to see if all was well. What would I do if I awakened next to my beloved Mommom's lifeless body one morning? If she wasn't in her bed, I would prowl the house until I saw a light on. (As an early riser, my grandmother would often be up before 4 AM having her quiet time with the Lord.) With the assurance that she was here another day I could go back to sleep until the morning sunlight entered the room.

Maturing into adulthood presented new opportunities for the specter of fear. I married my high school sweetheart, we had a family, and I was determined to break free from the worry that held me captive on so many fronts. However, in real life there was an ever-present possibility for anxiety to enter my world. I was powerless to change my thought process because my focus was always on me. I was constantly looking at myself and what would happen to me if…something happened to one of our children, or if my husband decided he wanted to do something "different" with his life like my father had done or this circumstance or that happened. I'm guessing you can fill in the blank several ways and it would apply because fear is experienced and understood, universally. We have concern over every area of life at one time or another from our family circumstances to global warming and the War on Terror. I wanted to be free from the things that were preventing joy in my life.

Professing to be Christian was not hard; but part of my struggle with sharing my faith journey is confessing that I did not begin maturing in my relationship with the Lord until late in life. Thanks to God, I belonged to a community of believers all of my life. The members of my church family planted seeds that were nurtured and have given roots to my belief in an all-powerful, loving God. Still, I had no real personal relationship with the Lord, and I wasn't free from fear. When I began to study the Word of God for myself, both in personal study and community Bible studies, the power to escape the grip that fear exercised over me became attainable. God used the unchangeable message of His living Word to grow my faith. In my meditations and prayer life He showed me His faithfulness in passages like 1Peter 5:7, *"Cast all your anxiety on Him because He cares for you,* Deuteronomy 31:8, *"The Lord Himself goes before you and will be with you; He will never leave you or forsake you. Do not be afraid; do not be discouraged."* Over and over His Word dismissed fear for His children: Abraham, Hagar, Moses, the people of Israel, Mary, Joseph, the Disciples of Christ, Paul and yes, even for me.

Am I fearless now? No, but I fear *less*. When adversity of any kind threatens to overcome my peace and rob me of my joy, I turn my eyes to the Lord and seek His comfort rather than relying on my feelings. My prayer over the past few years comes from the Psalms of David.

> *"Search me, O God, and know my heart; test me and know my anxious thoughts.*
> *See if there is any offensive way in me, and lead me in the way everlasting."* Psalm 139:23-24

God knows me. He loves me. He will never leave me or abandon me. He is the stronghold of my life—of whom (or what) shall I be afraid? In Him I now have the power to experience peace in the midst of fear.

Are you afraid?

Debbie Pearce

The Visit

I want to share a very sacred moment in my life. It's something that I rarely talk about because it is so personal, but I think it is fitting for this book of testimonials.

Back in the eighties, my life was in shambles. My business was failing, my marriage was failing and my faith had cratered. Being the arrogant person I was, it never entered my mind that I had brought a lot of this on myself. I felt God was dumping on me. I was depressed and was seeing a therapist when a friend gave me a book to read, <u>A ROOM CALLED REMEMBER</u>, by Frederick Buechner.

One night in 1984…actually, it was July 16…I was home alone. My wife was at some kind of a retreat for the weekend and the kids were off at camp. Sitting in my den and <u>drinking coffee</u>, I was re-reading the book, when a truth was revealed to me that led to an epiphany that changed my life.

I was on chapter two…Faith.

So, I got out my Bible and followed along in Hebrews 11. And there it was: The truth.

Scripture told about how Noah, Gideon, Abraham & Sarah, Moses and many other giants of the faith had been promised all sorts of things by God, but then God decided to do a new thing, sort of reneging on his original promise. As the author of Hebrews puts it, "These were all commended for their faith, yet none of them received what had been promised. <u>God had planned something better</u> for us so that only together with us would they be made perfect." The revelation to me from all this was that I was never a giant of the faith. And if these who had faithfully obeyed God yet were not presented with the "promise," who was I to assume that God should act differently to me? Then it hit me…like them, though as small as I was…God had something better in mind for me than anything I could even begin to comprehend. But it would only be by faith that I would be led to what that better thing was. And so, I was satisfied and relented.

And, at that moment, the Risen Christ stood before me.

I wish I could describe Him. I wish I could say what He was wearing and that I saw with my own eyes His wounds. Yet, all I know for sure was that I was in the presence of the holiest entity I have ever encountered. And we had a conversation. It wasn't casual, but it wasn't formal.

In some manner other than words I could plainly hear Him as He conveyed the charge that He wanted me to become a pastor, in His name. I spoke, but I don't remember whether or not I spoke out loud when I responded with something like: "Lord, I am a broken man. I am screwed up. My life is in a black hole. Obviously, You've made some sort of mistake."

And His answer to that was: "Perfect! You are exactly what I'm looking for!"

Four years later, in February, 1988, I entered the Presbyterian seminary at Austin. I was forty-seven years old, divorced, without a dime to my name. Three years later, I finished my studies while holding two jobs. In March of 1991, I was called to be the pastor of First Presbyterian Church of Kingsville, Texas and have served here ever since. After ten years of single-ness, I remarried in 1995. I am sixty-eight years old and have no thought of retiring. I waited this long to get going; I pray that I still have a ways to go before the Risen Lord is done with me.

I just celebrated the 25th anniversary of "The Visit." A day does not go by that I don't take time to thank God for his Amazing Grace that saved a wretch like me.

Chuck Miller

Thought for the Day

The Holy Spirit began to move in a powerful way in me in 2001. I had a burning desire to bring my daughter closer to Christ. She was 27 at the time and lived in Dallas. I began emailing her a "thought" I found every morning during my devotional time. At the end of that year I compiled every day into a book I called "Thought for the Day" and gave it to all my family members as a Christmas gift. That was the beginning of my biggest leap of faith and what has come to be over the past eight years my greatest joy—meeting my Lord early in the morning and feeling the power of the Holy Spirit work through me to reach others by emailing them a "Thought for the Day." I can't explain it, but through the joy of reading Scripture and books, I am able to find something that has meaning for me and that I can pass along to others. It is definitely not about me. I sometimes go back and reread something and wonder how I could have known those words were meant for me that day.

Yvonne Babbitt

The Body of Christ is ALIVE

I knew what I was about to do was wrong. Something inside of me was screaming at me to get up and walk out, but something else made me stay. Fear made me stay in that doctor's office and continue with the abortion. I let fear take over my life that day, yet somehow the Lord in his wisdom and love saw my pain, knew my choice, and had forgiven me long before I was willing to forgive myself. My abortion became the avenue by which the Lord would finally be able to get across to me.

A few days after the abortion, I was still in a daze as I graduated from college. To this day I don't even remember walking across the stage, because I was still in that doctor's office reliving my experience. I had convinced myself that I was Pro-Choice all my life and that the decision I had made was best for me and my only daughter. When people would ask, I would openly talk about my abortion, trying to convince myself that I wasn't evil. I tried to use logic and reason to justify an action that was purely emotional. Needless to say, all of that logic and reason went out the door when I finally let myself feel what I had done. I see now that the Lord had been trying to speak to me through the people in my life. Some of them were so upset at my decision that they made it a point to tell me (God bless their souls!). I tried to stay angry with them to keep the truth at bay.

One day I was visiting with a friend of mine and she insisted I get on this website called Rachel's Vineyard. I had some interest in getting help for the pain but I wasn't ready to go to church. I couldn't even sit through a mass without feeling an uncontrollable urge to leave. The need was overwhelming to just jump out of the pew and run full speed out the exit, leaving an "Amy shaped hole in the door." Still, against my objections my friend had me go to her apartment and get on the website. She was not willing to let me leave unless I filled out the application. Now, the woman is in a wheelchair, so there was no way I could disrespect her by just walking out. She had gone through so much in her own life, and to see her trying to help me was something not to be overlooked. So I filled out the application, thinking there was no way I would be able to go.

As the weeks progressed, I was hearing God calling me to His church by way of others. Slowly I would make my way to mass on Sundays and something just became alive at those celebrations. It was like being consumed with love and truth. The priest took an interest in my little family of two and others invited me to Bible study and RCIA classes. I became an active member for a while. Then I got the letter in the mail telling me that I had been given a scholarship to pay for my fees for the Rachel's Vineyard retreat. It was apparent that the Lord had something to tell me and that I was doing the right thing. Slowly things fell into place that month and I was soon on my way to a weekend I would never forget.

Rachel's Vineyard was such a wonderful experience in my life. The women I met there and the tears and love that were shared were the beginning of many blessings I would find in the arms of the Almighty and my church.

I wish I could say that the story ends there and that I became a "good Catholic girl," but that just isn't the case. Even now I am plagued by doubts and fears and evil thoughts that tell me to hurt myself, but I know the truth and I know that the Lord loves me.

The point of this testimony is that the Lord used everyone in my life to reach me. The Body of Christ is alive in all those people who answered His call, and even more so in the ones who didn't know they were doing the Lord's will. Most of all, the Body of Christ was working in all those people who stood up for their faith, acted on behalf of Christ, and brought me home.

Amy Suriz

It's not Your Fight

Out on a desolate, deserted, plain, I found myself all alone. Looking this way and that and forward and back, there was no one around. Tired and exhausted and just barely alive, I had chased the enemy for as long as I could remember. But I was now lost, tired, bruised and broken from past battles and life itself slipping out of me. Stumbling on I fell to my knees, vision blurring, eyes stinging, all my energy gone, my mind too about to give up. I hit the ground, facing forward, something appeared to be coming.

It was the enemy. Drawn out into the desert all alone, I had caught him. Or was it really that I had fallen into a trap. Lacking the energy to even raise my head, I no longer possessed the strength to keep my eyes open. Hearing the noise of a fast approaching army, that stretched from one end of the horizon to the other, my fate was sealed.

In my heart a cry for help was trying to make its way past my lips. But it seems I had waited too late to speak any words at all. My cry for help seemed trapped but somehow I released it with the passing of what remained of my breath. Like a whisper it went on its way.

My best guess was that a storm erupted the next moment. Winds began blowing, swirling, furious noises coming up from behind. Fast approaching and passing so close to me and then moving beyond, missing me completely. Nothing makes sense.

The next thing I know, I am surrounded by people, gently moving me and caring for me. After a drink and some time I feel my energy coming back. They assist me to my feet and look into my eyes. I break the silence and explain I am on a journey; an enemy to defeat is still before me. I hear their mumbled conversation, but can't make out a word. I think to ask how they were spared from the great storm that had passed by.

Storm? There was no storm. That was your Father's footprints as He passed by. He heard your call and came to save you from the enemy, one of them replied.

I decided it was time to rejoin the fight and told the group so. It's not your fight, they said in unison, you are the treasure of your Father, and He wants you to come home with us.

So it was that a son came home.

Ed Schetzsle

"I AM....."

When Moses asked God his name, God simply responded "I Am." Two of the simplest words in the English language, yet two of the most powerful words you can say. By responding with "I Am" God was saying that He is everything, all that exist is from Him and in Him.

How we finish the statement "I am ..." says a lot about our existence. Often you will hear people say "I am never going make it," or "I am not important." This negative self belief stands in the way of our reaching our full potential.

I have probably asked the question "Who Am I" hundreds of times. One day, in prayer, I received a clear message from God. He said, "You are my child and I love you." That day God made clear to me five affirmations of who I am. He told me that each one of us is significant, purposeful, and capable, a relational being, and a champion. These affirmations apply to each one of us.

I am significant - I believe one of the core desires in our hearts is to feel important. We want to know that our existence has meaning. God does not create accidents; He is intentional behind what He does. The very fact that you are alive says you are important to God. That alone should be enough to satisfy the desire of importance. Our egos seek out significance through our jobs, accumulation of objects, and the praise of others. None of these can show your true meaning and impact on the world. I was having trouble understanding how I could make an impact with my life. I then asked the question, "What if my wife wasn't there tomorrow, how would your life change?" Obviously I would be devastated and life would never be the same. Then I asked "How would the world be different if I was gone tomorrow?" This made me realize that every day I make an impact on my world through my job, my interaction with people, through every person I talk with and don't talk with. The simplest smile can make a difference. I began to understand the great opportunity each one of us has to impact those around us. Your meaning is in the way you live.

I Am Purposeful – The search for purpose has troubled man for thousands of years. I believe that there is one simple answer to the question "Why am I here?" The answer is to serve God and positively impact His kingdom. That is my purpose, your purpose, everyone's purpose. Where most of us get lost is the "How." God has put different passions in each one of our hearts, because each one of us will meet our purpose in different ways. We have unique sub-purposes. These sub-purposes will always work towards serving God and His kingdom. Sub-purposes will often change throughout your life. You may say, "I am only a student." If you are student, then that is your purpose. If you become a parent, that is another area in which God has given you a purpose. Wherever you are in life you can choose to find a purpose in it. I do believe that each one of us is called with unique passions and talents that God will use for His glory. Through the steps of our life journeys, we can find comfort in knowing that everything is orchestrated by our heavenly Father to fulfill His purpose. We must be open to fulfilling His mission for our lives.

I Am Capable - God will not ask you to do something that you are not capable of accomplishing. You have to believe that you are capable, because — guess what — you are. One of my favorite sayings is, "God does not call the prepared, He prepares the called." Every day of our lives we are being taught lessons to prepare us to fulfill our purposes. You may not feel as if you have the talent or training to do what He is asking. God will not give you a purpose without the capability to fulfill it. I love the story of King David. No one thought he was capable of killing Goliath, let alone being King. The training he received as a Shepherd prepared him to do both. Based on your experiences, your personality, your judgment, your passion, you can impact the world in a wholly unique way. This belief of being capable goes beyond talent. When God says you are capable, He is also referring to surviving life's struggles. It is through Him that we find this capability to persevere and become triumphant. There are situations in your life that you will face where you don't believe you'll make it or succeed. These are situations where God is putting together a plan where you will endure in a way that only He can get the glory. By falling into His arms we will gain more strength than one could ever imagine. Know that you are capable; you just need to trust and try.

I Am a Relational Being – the greatest causes of joy and pain in life stem from our relationships. God has built each one of us with a desire to love and be loved. The two most important relationships that we each have are our relationship with Jesus and the relationship with ourselves. These two relationships will affect all other relationships. I never truly understood the love God felt for us and the depth of the sacrifice He made through His son, until the day I first held my daughter. It was at that moment I could comprehend the sacrifice He made and how much He loves each one of us. By growing this relationship, the love God has for you will pour through you out onto the world. Take time to develop and nurture this relationship through prayer, study, and pure gratitude. Through this relationship you will better understand yourself. Treat everyone around you with the love and respect that God call us to. Though this is not always easy, it is essential to God's purpose for you.

I Am a Champion – There are two meanings to the word champion. One is to excel at something and the other is to fight for something. I believe that we are all called by God to excel in life and to fight for His kingdom. Through understanding your significance, discovering your purposes, using your capabilities, and strengthening your relationships, you will be living the life of a champion. When we look at the world's champions, we often look to people who are bold and confident, who have strong work ethic, someone who has that special quality. We look to athletes and other celebrities as examples of champions. The truth is; champions exist all around us. Each one of us has that special quality it takes to be a champion because we have God. He wants you to excel in all that you do each day for His glory and to impact His kingdom. I believe these five affirmations are applicable to each area of your life, from your personal to your business life. God wants you to know that you will and already do make a difference in his kingdom. You are truly capable of changing your world for the better. Whenever you begin to doubt who you are, look in the mirror and say, "I am significant. I am purposeful. I am capable. I am a relational being. I am a champion!" Today is the day to begin living like the champion you are.

Joseph M. Cortez

Miracles from Heaven

When my grandson was only four years old, he and his two-year-old step sister were abandoned by his mother hundreds of miles away in Arkansas. They were left with a family who were about to be given custody by the court. The grandparents for his little sister from Wichita, Kansas were called. Somehow they got my number and called me, and asked me if I was willing to take him, and I responded YES! I called his sister's other grandparents too, to see if they could take my grandson while I made arrangements for him.

I was devastated about the situation and had to think quickly. I prayed and cried to get an answer. About three months earlier, I had met a lady whose sister lived in Wichita, so I rushed to her to see if she was planning to go up to Wichita. She said, "No, but my sister is coming down today." They agreed to bring my grandson down with them and I made the necessary arrangements to make sure that my grandson could be picked up and delivered to them as soon as possible. Time was of the essence, I desperately needed to get him to Wichita before they left for Texas.

It was getting late when I heard my friend's sister tell her that her son had developed a toothache and would not be leaving until the following day so they could see a dentist. What a blessing, I thought. That gave my grandson a chance to make it back with them. It was not until 10 p.m. but he made it. Had his little sister's grandparents not picked them up, the court would have had to make a custody decision on this the next day.

It was absolutely miraculous, this miracle worked like a puzzle that came into place perfectly. Whenever I told anyone about this I could not hold back my tears. This was only one of so many miracles I have experienced in my life, but it was the most meaningful and beautiful.

Yes, amazingly, miracles do happen, and it is such a great feeling. My faith and prayers have kept me believing in wonderful outcomes. My grandson is now 17 years old and a senior in high school. I pray that his dream to go to college comes true.

Irene Cipriano

I Will Give You Rest

"Come to me, all you who are weary and burdened, and I will give you rest." Matthew 11:28

On a Saturday during which my wife had to work a 12-hour shift, I was a bit upset that I would have to spend the entire day alone. I intentionally slept late, took my time getting dressed, and drove in to town to shop and purchase some items I needed for a ministerial event the following weekend. I intentionally used-up as much time as I could, but soon was bored with unproductive wandering. When it was close enough to lunch time, I drove to a restaurant so I could make a mess in someone else's kitchen instead of my wife's. I was not pleased, however, because I have much disdain for eating alone.

I found a table in the back which allowed me to hide in shame of being alone for lunch. I placed my lunch on the table, sat down, and prayed a prayer of discontent...without even realizing I was doing that. When I concluded my prayer and took my first bite of lunch, my attention was directed to some hand movement off to my right and slightly in front of me. I studied the very odd, very intentional hand movements of a man, and then, in a moment of surprise, I realized that the hand movement was that of a man who is a deaf/mute. In that short moment of surprise, I realized that the deaf/mute was praying...praying before he, too, began to eat lunch. At that realization, and in only a few seconds, my emotions changed from discontent to shame. I was ashamed because I realized that I have been blessed with so much, and yet I sat at a table loaded with food and prayed a prayer of discontent to the same God of the universe to which the deaf/mute was praying a prayer of thanksgiving. I stopped, prayed again, and asked for forgiveness.

As I changed my focus from my loneliness to my blessings, God turned my discontent to peace. God had given me a gift...the gift of rest. I had not known before that rest does not just come when I recline or lie down, but when I am suspended...cradled...by the peace that passes all understanding. Thank the Lord for His gift of rest.

Prayer: Father God, thank you for rocking me in the cradle of your love, even during the middle of a busy day, as you deliver your gift of rest.

Focus: All of us who need to be reminded that rest is a gift of God which He delivers in several forms.

Jonathan Ibarra

Don't Worry, Be Happy

Are you a worrier? I come from a long line of worriers. I think worrying came through my grandmother Lucy and she passed it down to all five of her daughters, including my mother. When I was a little girl I learned quickly that the way you knew Mama Lucy really loved one of her children or grandchildren was that she worried about them. She had a lot of them to worry about – ten children and 24 grandchildren. In my grandmother's world there was always someone to worry about and she literally worried herself sick about them. I think my grandmother invented the shingles and stomach ulcers.

I guess you could say my tendency to worry comes naturally. Do you know there is actually a gene that has been implicated in producing chronic worriers? That news made the front page of the New York Times in 1996. A particular gene has been linked to individuals who are prone to anxiety, pessimism and negative thinking. So perhaps I am a *born* worry wart.

I bet you worry occasionally, too. What kinds of things do we worry about? Our health? Our finances? What about our families? Evidently worry is an almost universal problem. Amazon lists thousands of book titles on the subject of worry. Clearly I'm not alone. Even the Bible says more about fear than about heaven. But let's just admit it - most of what we worry about will never happen. And the things that do happen - we can't change them by worrying about them. Worry, fear and regret do a lot of damage in our lives - physically, emotionally and spiritually. I cannot do anything to change the past, but I *can* ruin the present by worrying about the future.

The Bible has a lot to say about worry. One of the most practical instructions is in Philippians 4:6-8. Paul the apostle says, *"Do not be anxious about anything, but in everything, by prayer and petition, with thanksgiving, present your request to God. And the peace of God, which transcends all understanding, will guard your hearts and your minds in Christ Jesus."* What if we took this instruction to heart and put it into practice? What if we handed that worrisome situation over to God in prayer and thanked Him for taking care of it? Paul says in verse seven, if we begin to live this way we will experience amazing peace – a kind of peace we can't even imagine. In verse eight, Paul tells us what to think about instead of our worries – "whatever is true, whatever is noble, whatever is right, whatever is pure, whatever is lovely, whatever is admirable – if anything is excellent or praiseworthy – think about such things." Many things can fall into these categories, but Christ's peace underlies them all. This is not just positive thinking; this is a mind captive to Christ. This kind of thinking brings peace and contentment to me. Contentedness is not something that comes when I no longer have uncertainty in life. That day will never come. Instead I experience peace as I become prayerful and thankful, practice spiritual thinking and trust Christ with my life and my future.

Can I really trust the Lord to look after my best interests? I've never really had a terrible tragedy happen in my life. What if the worst should happen? Will God be there for me? How do I know I can really give my cares to God and rest in His provision? God's Word provides numerous examples in both the Old and New Testaments of people who went through situations where they had reason to be very worried. Yet their stories bear out the faithfulness of God in protecting them and bringing them through the trials they faced.

For some first-hand witnesses, I can look to the challenges and tragedies experienced by my brothers and sisters in the Body of Christ, people who have lost spouses and children, battled cancer and heart disease, struggled with chronic illness and disabilities, experienced financial catastrophes – you name it. And yet all of them stand before me as proof that God's grace sees us through the worst that can happen. They are witnesses that God stood by them, comforted them and led them. Jesus held their hands and wiped their tears through the trauma and the pain of the worst life can throw our way and gave them the peace that passes understanding, the conviction that all things would somehow work together for good. What better proof do I need than that? God prepared all these brothers and sisters to help show all of us worriers the way to peace.

Today I'm turning all my fears and worries over to God. I can't fix a single thing by worrying about it – but He can fix anything because *"...nothing is impossible for God"* Luke 1:37

Susan Lewis

God's Rain

I was 15, possibly barely 16. It was a Saturday. I was alone. I had no drivers' license. I had no car. I had an appointment at my drama teacher's apartment that morning. She lived about two miles from my house. The only way I had to get there was on my bicycle. About half an hour before the appointment, it started to rain. Hard. Really hard. The kind of rain that makes you feel wet in your soul just looking at it through the window. The kind that you can't run through or walk through or hide from. All you can do is surrender. Either stay inside . . . or get completely soaked. Those are your options. That was the kind of rain I saw that day.

This made me very upset. I had no car . . . no license . . . no friends . . . no family to help me get where I needed to go. Oh, the misery! Remember, I was only 15 or 16 at the time. After wallowing in self-pity for several minutes, a thought occurred to me as I gazed out the window at the torrents. I remembered the story of Noah's ark and that God made it rain for forty days and forty nights. If He could do that,

He could also make it stop raining. That is . . . if He wanted to.

So I prayed. I asked God to make it stop raining. Of course, before that I asked God to forgive me for my sins and for Jesus to be my Lord and Savior . . . for the 15th time . . . just in case. Then I took my bicycle and stood under the carport and waited for the rain to stop. I waited. I waited some more. Nothing happened. I remembered that the Bible said that God did not hear the prayers of people who had sin hidden in their hearts. After waiting for several minutes, I eventually concluded that God had not heard my prayer or maybe didn't care, probably because I was a bad kid or had committed some terrible sin. Again, remember that I was only 15 or 16. But are any of us any different as adults? Don't we all constantly draw conclusions about the extent of God's love and power based on the things that do or do not happen the way we want them to in life?

After some time, I made the decision to ride my bike to my teacher's apartment anyway. I knew that I would get completely soaked. "Oh, well," I thought. If God did not care about me getting soaking wet, then why should I?

The next moment took my breath away. It stopped raining.

Can you hear me say that? The very second that I pushed my foot on the pedal and came out from under the corrugated-tin roof of my parents' carport — it stopped raining! Completely! In one split second, it went from cats-and-dogs-raining-buckets-in-torrents to blue-sky-dry-as-a-bone. Oh, sure, the pavement was still wet, but I managed to ride my bicycle the entire two miles to my teacher's apartment without getting hit by a single drop of rain.

I knew that God had performed a miracle for me and answered my prayer. I was shocked. I'm sure I did not know what to think. I was too grateful and ecstatic to think. I vaguely recall thinking something like, "Oh, Wow. There really is a God!" Oh, how my spirit soared that day. I felt as if I was riding on a cloud. I arrived at my teacher's apartment and rehearsed there for a few hours. At the end of rehearsal, I rode my bicycle back home, enjoying the memory of how God had delivered me that morning.

What happened next removed any doubt that the hand of God was truly upon me. I arrived back at my parents' house and the very instant that the back wheel of my bicycle rolled under the carport, it started raining again! The skies opened up and poured down rain all around me, every bit as hard as it had been raining that morning.

For many years I would remember that day. I wish I could say that my faith grew tremendously as a young man because of that incident. I wish I could say that I became a devoted follower of Jesus Christ at that very moment and that my heart was completely turned over to God. But I would be lying. I did try to be a better Christian for a few months after that. I took my Bible with me to school and went to the library to read during lunch instead of going the cafeteria. It didn't last long. That was my sopho-more year in high school and it only took a couple of months for a few things to not work out the way

I wanted them to for me to lose interest in the things of God. After high school, I wholeheartedly rebelled against God and the church. In fact, from the time I was 18 until I was almost 30, I did not pray, read the Bible or go to church even once voluntarily.

Why? How can that be? How could I see such a mighty move of God on my behalf and then turn away from God so soon thereafter? The Israelites did the same thing. They walked on dry land between two walls of water piled thousands of feet high into the air. They saw God deliver them from the armies of Pharaoh. Two weeks later they were worshiping the golden calf. Why? I think for two reasons. First, their hearts were still in slavery. Their physical lives had been delivered, but their hearts had not. Second, they were bored. It is easy to cry out to God in desperation when we are in the middle of the battle. We tend to lose our need for God when we are bored.

In spite of my rebellion, I always regarded that memory with fondness. I even shared that story with a few close friends. During those years in college, law school and the workplace, I met many people who would have loved to convince me that there was no God. I knew better. I may have decided that He didn't love me or didn't want me or that I did not want Him. But I knew He was there. There was no way that I could become an atheist after experiencing something like that.

Years later I would come to understand a deeper meaning to that story. God used that event to demonstrate the power of faith. As long as I was waiting for it to stop raining, it didn't. But as soon as I stopped waiting and came out from under the shed, it stopped raining. That is a picture of faith. The Jordan River stopped at the very moment that the children of Israel stepped into the rushing river . . . and it started flowing again the moment they reached the other side.

God wants us to believe that He will come through for us even before we see any sign or evidence of that beforehand. He loves it when we take the first step . . . make the first move. Not out of haste or arrogance, but out of a calm and steady assurance that we know God is for us and with us.

When I was 29, I attended the Walk to Emmaus, a Christian retreat, and met Jesus . . . again . . . for the first time. During the closing ceremony, I reflected back on my earlier experimentations with faith and realized that they were just that. I had never really made a bold full-fledged commitment to Christ. I knew that day that if I wanted my relationship with Christ to be different this time, I was going to have to make an all-out commitment and stop caring what other people thought. So when I was given my chance, I took the microphone and announced, sobbing and weeping, to the people gathered there, "This weekend brought an end to twelve years of separation from Christ. And now I am going to study and meditate and pray and surround myself with Christian friends . . . and I am going to walk with Jesus until He comes back to bring me home."

After the retreat, I continued to exercise my faith. I soon realized that I would have to start praying and reading my Bible even when I didn't "feel" like it or when I couldn't "hear" God talking to me. Guess what. After about three or four days, I did "feel" like reading the Bible and I could "hear" God talking to me. Then I applied those same principles to tithing and sharing my faith. I tithed when I didn't have the money and shared my faith when I didn't know how people would respond. That's how it works. God demonstrates His power little by little . . . "from faith to faith" as the Bible says in Romans.

A few years later, after I'd seen God put my life back together — and take it apart again-I realized an even deeper meaning to that story, that miracle, that God performed for me as a teenage boy. God loved me. Of all the prayers that were being lifted up that day, He heard mine . . . and He cared. He wanted to show Himself strong on my behalf that day. Of all the problems in the world that needed to be solved that day, God still had time to listen and care about whether a 15-year old boy got wet riding his bike to school. It is still sometimes hard for me to accept that meaning, that message. It took me a long time for my mind to open up to that message. It has taken my heart even a little longer. But I desperately need to remember that. We all do. God cares about the little things. And He doesn't keep it a secret. All He is looking for is a little faith.

CRA

A Real Relationship

I've been going to church all my adult life; there's something about being married in a church that drew me there. I made a solemn promise and meant to keep it.

As our family grew, we all attended church; that's just what the Bridgeman family did on Sunday. Like a lot of us, being active in church was part of my life, but I didn't respond to the call for a personal relationship with Christ.

My carefully cultivated life began to unravel when a series of circumstances led me to the difficult decision to divorce my husband of almost 28 years. I was ashamed and felt like I was breaking my promise to God, so I no longer attended church.

Life continued, but I was not back in church. I had spent most of my adult life in California where people change spouses almost as often as they change cars, but this is Texas – part of the Bible belt. People don't get divorced in Texas, right?

Our church was beginning the Purpose Driven Life program and I went back to church and joined a small group for the PDL study. As we introduced ourselves, I took a deep breath and expressed that I was going through a difficult divorce. Imagine my surprise to have everyone there express support for me. I feared their reaction, but didn't need to.

The study and support of my small group became essential as I navigated the waters of selling the home, taking care of the children and living on my own. They cried with me when I stumbled. The sorrow of my loss was almost more than I could bear – it was more than I could bear alone, but then I remembered that I was not alone.

This was the second time God had wooed me and this time I wholeheartedly accepted. Matthew 10:35-37 from The Message says: *I've come to cut—make a sharp knife-cut between son and father, daughter and mother, bride and mother-in-law—cut through these cozy domestic arrangements and free you for God. Well-meaning family members can be your worst enemies. If you prefer father or mother over me, you don't deserve me. If you prefer son or daughter over me, you don't deserve me.*

The marriage that was leading me away from God ended. It had given me three beautiful children but in its state, at the end, it was leading me away from God.

Life is sometimes difficult, like when my ex-husband passed away in December in New York, but the joy that God has given me, more than replaces the sorrow of my loss. I wouldn't change a minute of the new life He has given me.

We serve an awesome God who cares about everything in our lives, but he is a jealous God. I thank him daily for walking with me when I lost the things I treasured and then giving me something far better – a real relationship with the One who loves me more than anyone ever has and more than anyone ever will.

Gale Bridgeman

The Capitulation

I grew up in Orange, Texas attending the Presbyterian Church. God was a Being out in the regions found in the Bible, Sunday School, conversations of adults, etcetera. I knew about God the Father, Jesus His Son, and the Holy Spirit, but a personal relationship was not present. I see God's hand in my younger life now, in the blessings of family, solid parents, teachers in various church activities, and some of my friends. God was there and I was His child but I am not sure when the "threshold" of being saved was crossed. By this, I mean the point where if I had died, it would have been up and on to heaven.

Presbyterian kids join the church as members at or after the age of 12. After taking a series of 5 or 6 classes led by an elder or pastor, one becomes a member. The understanding of God was limited but still I joined the church after completing the classes and standing in front of the congregation while confessing a 12-year-old's understanding of sin, salvation and God. This understanding was extremely limited, but how much more do I know

now of God's total being, percentage-wise, than I did then? Not much. I believe the salvation was there in God's eyes because He sees the entire scan of time instantaneously. This salvation has been "a done deal" since before the foundation of the world.

Anyhow, childhood was chock full of many good times. We were comfortably middle class and my Mom made sure my sister and I were involved with lots of fun things. My Dad and I have a wonderful relationship. This was helped by his including me in lots of fishing, golfing, camping, hunting, and sports activities. I cherished our relationship and wanted to have a similar relationship with my own son(s).

In college I met Laura, the future Mrs. Hood. We were alike spiritually; faith was like a tattoo which one doesn't show, unless it is specifically mentioned (of course our faith, like the explosion in popularity of tattoos, is much more readily apparent nowadays). We were married the last year of college, the year before the start of dental school. She agreed to attend Presbyterian-type churches although her Southern Baptist background made some things a bit different at first (such as music which sounds like a funeral dirge, not saying "amen" out loud, and a typically older congregation). We attended church fairly regularly but pretty much lived for ourselves. Our first child, Lyle, was born during my last year of dental school. It was a difficult time in many ways. Things were tight financially (although Laura kept us comfortable working for IBM), school was diffi- cult, and the marriage relationship was ok but not without lots of bickering. There was also the adjustment of a new mouth to feed (along with him being a somewhat difficult child to rear), and the difficulty of making good enough grades to get into a residency program.

We slogged through dental school, a residency, and a move to Atlanta, Georgia. Things were progressing but not great overall. I felt like something was not right nor were the relationships at home right. I had usually accomplished the goals in life by determination, hard work, study, and force of will. The family relationships were not improving despite my efforts. Unfortunately, I was harsh, selfish, critical, prideful, etcetera.

In Atlanta I met some good solid Christians. One was a fellow periodontist who was a mentor both spiritually and professionally. A second dentist was also a good Christian whose faith in Jesus was a strong part of his character. Neither man broadcast his faith but both seemed to model it in attitude and behavior. There were other influences such as a prayer meeting, where earnest prayers were offered which did not sound hokey or perfunctory. The periodontal mentor lent me a 3-volume set of books on the Gospel of John to read. It was overkill, but I dutifully read them and was convicted that things were not right with God. The conviction of the Holy Spirit was present in many ways: dissatisfaction with family relationships, difficulty in getting started professionally, conviction while reading the books on John, etcetera.

We returned to Corpus Christi after one year in Georgia (pronounced "Joe-jah") after both going through tough times professionally. However, God used these tough times in positive ways. The personal relationships, especially the one with the smart but hard-headed and limit-pushing son, were still not excellent. The Holy Spirit was working on both of us, but especially me. I tried reading the Bible a few times (had a much better understanding of John!), but did not get much out of it. We continued to attend church sporadically. Jesus was our Savior but the Lordship thing was like a buffet, we picked what we wanted. Most of the buffet items were left unpicked, thank you.

In 1991, Dr. Todd Howell invited me to a Christian Business Men's Committee luncheon. A former astronaut, Charlie Duke, was the speaker. He told about his life concerning professional accomplishments with NASA and going to the moon on an Apollo Mission. He also relayed that his family relationships were not nearly so stellar. His wife was ready to sock him to the moon using divorce papers and his kids hated him. He told about a time when he was with his son and how his son flinched like he might get smacked when Charlie reached up to straighten his own hair. This really hit home as there had been a similar flinching experience with my own son, Lyle. That speech helped crystallize my misery, and how inept my efforts were proving to be. Charlie led a prayer at the end and I capitulated to God. My "uncle" to the Father caused a weight to be lifted. The lordship of Keith ended officially (the Lord Keith movement keeps trying to resurrect, unfortunately). Jesus was my Savior and Lord.

Bible study was no longer a drag. There were CBMC Bible studies and another at my church, Grace Presbyterian in Corpus Christi. The family relationships slowly began to improve. The old harsh, volatile, critical, vain, haughty, and selfish ways did not shrink significantly overnight but they did start to slooooooowly shrink. Good solid Christians like Greg Hood and Don Arvin led studies. Being around other mature and/or growing Christians greatly helped. Laura was slow at first to come along but she soon joined and was likewise given a new Hood Ornament concerning Lordship for guidance. Our relationship, as well as those of Lyle and his siblings, Josie, Leroy and Alex, are much better. In every way, it has been a wonderful capitulation.

Keith Hood

Surrender, Seek and Serve

Growing up in the church made accepting God easy. I have to admit that there were times when I wondered if believing in God would turn into a "Laura, there really isn't a Santa Claus" moment.

At the age of 19, as I went off to college for the first time, it occurred to me that Christianity was finally my choice. No one could make me go to church. That understanding caused me to love God more than ever.

Like most college students, however, I eventually became so preoccupied with my freedom and attracted to sin that I was willing to give up my commitment to Christ.

My downward spiral didn't involve drugs, alcohol or any of the "unacceptable sins." Life did, however, no longer revolve around my relationship to Christ.

I spent the rest of the next 20 years in a compartmentalized life. I was in church on Sunday... hiding in the pews. I would run out of church the minute it was over. There was no willingness to build

Christian relationships. I know now that I was afraid the "real" Christians would see through my mask of Christianity.

I turned to success as a way to feel fulfilled. Maybe if I proved myself at work I would feel better. Being successful in my career provided occasional temporary satisfaction. Through my accomplishments I was able to convince myself that life wasn't so bad.

Over time my selfish behavior resulted in struggles that convinced me that I no longer deserved God's forgiveness. Many times I tried very hard to stop sinning so that I could feel worthy of the relationship with God that I missed so much. Many times I promised God that I would get close to Him again as soon as I "got myself straightened out."

It took me years of tears to realize that I was not capable of "getting right" on my own. My anxiety over trying and failing pulled me even farther away from God, and increased my insecurities.

A second failed marriage was the defining moment in my life. There was no more pretense of having it all together. No business accomplishments could overshadow the fact that my personal life was a mess.

Complete and utter surrender for me came in three stages:

<u>Surrendering to Him</u> – In a rock-bottom moment I had to admit to God that I had made a mess and nothing I could do would ever fix it. There had to be a moment when I was willing to beg Him to show

me what the next step was. I clung to Proverbs 3:5-6 through this stage.

<u>Seeking Him</u> – Eventually I realized that there would be no lasting peace unless I forgave myself and began to cherish my time alone with God. He wanted my everyday, ordinary life. I clung to Romans 12:1-2 (MSG Version) throughout this stage.

<u>Serving Him</u> – Finally I learned that the fastest way to get over my feelings of unworthiness was to expend energies on loving others. God gave us clear guidelines in Matthew 22:36-39. We are to love Him first and others second. Clinging to God and sharing the love I felt because of Him became natural.

There are still days when I struggle with depending on myself instead of God. When I realize I have once again taken control of my life away from God it humbles me immediately. I am reminded to Surrender, Seek, and Serve all over again.

It is in those moments that I remember the Message version of Romans 8:15-17…

"This resurrection life you received from God is not a timid, grave-tending life. It's adventurously expectant, greeting God with a childlike "What's next, Papa?" God's Spirit touches our spirits and confirms who we really are. We know who He is, and we know who we are: Father and children. And we know we are going to get what's coming to us—an unbelievable inheritance! We go through exactly what Christ goes through. If

we go through the hard times with Him, then we're certainly going to go through the good times with Him!"

I thank God for this new life. It is adventurous and I am grateful to be able to look up and say, "What's next, Papa?"

Laura Harris

John 8:32
**_"Then you will know the truth and the
truth will set you free."_**

My fortieth birthday fell on a Sunday. The night
before, my husband had given me a wonderful
surprise celebration with family and friends. It was a
very happy occasion but I didn't feel very happy on the
inside. On the outside I had everything going for me –
a loving husband, three beautiful children, and a nice
lifestyle - but on the inside, I had a powerful feeling
of longing and depression. And I felt really guilty for
feeling that way. How could I feel depressed when I
had been given so much? What was wrong with me? I
couldn't face going to church the next day. There were
so many people at my church who were on fire about
their faith and full of joy. I didn't want to be around all
those happy people who had something I wanted and
didn't know how to get. But God knew what was in
my heart and He started calling me, gently. Over the
next few months, I enrolled in a Bible study, I volun-
teered to help teach my son's Sunday school class,
and I signed up to go on a Walk to Emmaus.

The Walk to Emmaus is a four-day spiritual
renewal retreat. It was while I was there that I got

honest with God. The first night, I poured out my heart to Him, silently, privately, in the dark. I confessed my doubts and asked that if Jesus truly was the Son of God who died for my sins that He would let me know. And He did! I experienced the presence of the Holy Spirit in a powerful, physical way. It was like a cool, pleasant tingling all over my body. I was overcome by a sense of love, peace and assurance.

God turned my life around that weekend. He gave me a hunger and a passion for His Word. I wanted to know God. I read the Bible like it was a personal love letter written to me. I believed what God said was true – that not only did He have unconditional love for me but for everyone! That we can never fully grasp how much He loves us! He doesn't want anyone to perish! His thoughts and ways are higher than ours! He can do immeasurably more than we can ask or imagine! He has plans to give us hope and a future – eternal life with Him! He forgives our sins! If we seek Him with all our hearts, we will find Him! I believed all these wonderful things and God has shown me time and time again that He is true to His Word and His Word is true.

I started reading scriptures, meditating on them, memorizing them, and applying them to my life. One of my many favorite scriptures was (and is), *"if anyone is in Christ, he is a new creation; the old has gone and the new has come!"* 2 Cor 5:17 Now that is really good news for someone like me who wants to be changed by God! I had struggled with insomnia all my adult life and I really thought that as a new creation, my sleep problem would go away.

I didn't have any trouble going to sleep, but I would frequently wake up at 2:00, 3:00 or 4:00, toss and turn, try to go back to sleep, and sometimes get up to read a book. Well that "old" problem did not go away – I still wake up early. But as a new creation, I have a new perspective and a new plan of action. When I wake up, I get up and pray and read the Bible. I look forward to my extended quiet time with God. It is then that I most often get "holy nudges" to write someone, call someone, or do something for someone. God took what I thought was a weakness (my insomnia) and turned it around to be His strength.

I am a new creation when I choose to remain in Christ's love, but it is still a choice – a day-to-day and often moment-to-moment choice. Although I fail frequently and I am in daily need of God's grace, I can claim that His grace is sufficient for me. When I focus on the love and compassion of Christ, and stay centered in the truth of God's Word, I no longer focus on myself and all my failures, faults, and inadequacies. I am just an ordinary person but in Christ, I live an extraordinary, abundant life! It is a life of freedom - a life of love, joy, peace and purpose. In my walk with God over the last fourteen years, He has enabled me to do what I could not do on my own. He has given me more and blessed me more than I could ask or imagine. He has brought me out of the darkness and into His wonderful light in fellowship with Him and others. Thanks be to God for His indescribable gift!

Lorraine Volk

Wounded Healer

When I was asked to write my testimony, I first thought that it would be difficult to do, but then I realized that it's quite simple when it comes to expressing the goodness and love of God!

I had always known that God existed but I had not allowed Him into my life; even so, He kept drawing me closer to Him over the years - patiently and lovingly.

When I became a mother, I experienced all of the hormone imbalances that can occur, but there were nightmarish flashbacks too vivid to be unreal, and thence I began my journey into deep depression, detachment, and numbness. I had reached a very dark and desperate place, and nothing worldly worked. Yes, there are physicians and medicines that have been created by the grace of God, but these were not the answer for my downward, inward spiral. By the wonderful presence of the Holy Spirit He ever so gently led me to realize that I had wrongfully blamed God for painful things that had happened to me as a child. He showed me that as I cried those deeply painful, silent tears, He was there crying with me. I have come to know God as my Father, and Jesus as the lover of my soul, and I have complete trust in them, and I am now feeling unspeakable joy in my Godly womanhood! Did this happen overnight? By all means, no! It takes time and lots of courage to heal.

We all have horrible things happen to us, some by our own choices, but most at the hands of someone else; regardless of the situation, all pain is the same - dark, deep, and life-stealing. But there is hope: hope in the One and Only Jesus! He came to our world to save us from sin, and to bring us home to God when we are done; He mends and heals broken hearts and minds; He takes what is ugly and tarnished and turns them into brand new vessels. When we give Him our hurts and share with others our brokenness, not only does it give hope to others, but our hurt itself becomes an offering to the Lord, and it loses its stronghold on our lives. I recently was at a meeting and a young mother with a similar abusive background gave her testimony, and as I watched her give her tender memories, I could not help but think, "That was me 13 years ago." And once again, I remember how far my Jesus has brought me! I will always remember the first time that I received my "testimony," but I've come to understand that as we follow Jesus, not only do our hearts and lives change, but our testimony does as well - it doesn't stay the same! The women that so lovingly guided me when I first started my faith journey hold very special places in my heart, and now that I'm so in love with

Jesus, He is transforming me to become one of those women to others.

So, my dearest Tamara & Taylor, hang on to all that you know about the love of God during this difficult time. He is with you at every moment, especially when you feel that he doesn't hear or see your silent tears. HE IS WITH YOU – EMMANUEL - GOD WITH US! You are loved by an amazing God, and many, many wounded healers are praying on your behalf…

Amanda Elizardo Mendez

Truly Free

I was born In Toronto, Canada on October of 1981, and raised as a Roman Catholic. My whole life I have always felt very different from everyone else. I had a great zest for life, and an imagination that took me to places good and bad. I was someone who was viewed as a free spirit because I did what I wanted, dressed how I wanted, expressed myself, and stood strong on the belief of being true to yourself no matter what the cost. This type of attitude got me a lot of praise as well as a lot of difficulties in my life. On one hand, I was praised for many things like my dancing, writing, my appearance, and my ability to express myself; however I was ostracized by my peers, teased and tormented by my own thoughts. My mind often raced ahead of me and it affected my academics, social life, household chores, sleep, and my general mental health. I was diagnosed at a young age with ADD and suffered for many years with chronic insomnia, anxiety, panic attacks, and depression, but above all things I seemed to feel like I was being attacked. In 2004, I came to a point in my life where I had everything that would make most people happy. I had gotten married to the man of my dreams, had a beautiful home, a rising career in social work, and I felt completely beautiful on the outside. However on the inside I was falling apart. It is considerably worse when you have everything society views necessary to make you happy and complete and you still feel like there is something missing.

As a result of this feeling I went extremely downhill. I cut off all my hair, worshiped false idols, was frustrated and physically angry at my husband all the time, lost a lot of weight, smoked, drank, and was dangerously addicted to sleeping pills. In the middle of the night sometimes I would even wake up in complete fear and felt that something was hanging over me. My life was a mess and I badly wanted to end it. If I have everything I am supposed to have to make me happy, why do I feel like this??? I figured there was just no hope.

One day my best friend Chantelle encouraged me to attend a Christian church she attended regularly named Orangeville Baptist Church. She took me to a Christian book store and bought me a book and a bookmark with the quote Isaiah 40:31 *"Those that hope in the Lord will renew their strength. They will soar on wings like eagles."*

When I entered the church the people appeared to be so happy and so nice. It was very awkward for me to see people so happy. I sat beside a lady and she had a Bible cover that had the same Isaiah 40:31 quote on it. I thought to myself... is God trying to say something to me here? The sermon started and he was discussing spiritual warfare. On the projector screen beside him the same quote from Isaiah 40:31 was on display. As the pastor began to speak he talked about "the devil" and how he torments us through our thoughts and wants nothing but to steal our joy. When the pastor said this I could not believe it...... there was an awakening in my soul. I could not believe that this whole time, 24 years, that it was not my fault that these things were happening to me, but that there was something spiritual controlling my thoughts and literally attacking me. At that moment I felt as if a light was coming slowly over my body and this heaviness seemed to just literally be lifting off me. As tears uncontrollably came from my eyes Chantelle looked at me and said "Are you ok? What's wrong?" I smiled and said "I don't know. I feel so light and happy and free like I'm flying." Two people touched my shoulder from behind me and gently whispered that I had just received the Holy Spirit. "Well what does that mean? Why do I feel so happy?" They said, "You will see, God will show you."

As the service ended I glanced back at the screen at the Isaiah quote 31 *"Those that hope in the Lord will renew their strength. They will soar on wings like eagles."* And that is exactly how I felt that whole day, as if I was flying like an eagle. As dusk approached and I was getting ready for bed, I decided that I wanted to do things differently. I had been diagnosed with a sleeping condition where I was told I would need to take meds my whole life. My normal routine consisted of taking sleeping pills and fighting an overwhelming fear for several hours before I would finally rest for a total of usually seven to ten minutes a night, leaving me irritable and restless.

I decided to flush my pills down the toilet, and hold a rosary in my hands that night. As the familiar fear came over me I decided to say aloud "I know who you are and I believe in Jesus, He does not give me a spirit of fear but a spirit of sound mind." The thoughts in my mind began to slowly fade, and for the first time in 24 years I finally slept in peace. It has been three years since that night, and I have slept every night in peace. The journey I took from that day has done nothing more than completely transform me. In the last three years Jesus has transformed me, through His Word, from fear, humility, addictions, and lust, with patience, love, and forgiveness and I know this is only the beginning. A few years ago I was seen as someone who was free because of how I expressed myself, but I was never free. I was held captive in my mind and my own thoughts of what it meant to be free. But I now know the truth; now I am free. *"I can do everything through Him who gives me strength."* Philippians 4:13

Christina Yacoub

Ordinary is Amazing

As I grew up, my parents taught me about God, took me to church, and to Sunday school. It never occurred to me to question the existence of God. I just believed. I believed that Jesus died on a cross and rose again in three days.

When I was twelve I went to a Christian camp for a week. During one of our Bible lessons a man, whom I've never seen again, began to teach about Jesus. He spoke of Jesus' life, death and resurrection with such passion and power that I was overwhelmed. Jesus became real in my heart that day. However, I continued to just go through the motions of going to church and Sunday school each week.

As I journeyed into adulthood – high school, college, marriage to a military officer, and military life – I quit going through the motions. There was no traumatic exit, I just gradually lost focus. I still believed, but my walk was far from God.

When I was 24 years old and living in Alabama, God began to get my attention. I was battling infertility. I began praying fervently and asking "Where are you, God? Why aren't You answering my prayers?"

A year later, the fertility pills, testing and emotional stresses were taking their toll. For the first time in my life, I fell to my knees and cried out to the Lord.

By the grace of God, I became pregnant within a few months. Amazingly God blessed me with a child in spite of the fact that I still wasn't walking a daily journey with Him. I wasn't growing or being transformed by the truth. However, that precious baby got me back into the motions.

I was blessed with two more children. One Sunday I went to a special church service and I was convicted that I wasn't right with God. I began to thirst for knowledge of my Savior. I was tired of going through the motions. I longed for a personal relationship. I could no longer live off of everyone else's knowledge, faith and traditions. I had to know Christ; I longed to know what HE said, what HE taught and I wanted HIM, the Great Teacher, to teach me. I sat through that entire service and prayed "Jesus, come into my heart and teach me. Jesus, come into my heart and teach me."

Well, you can imagine what kind of journey began after praying that prayer over and over for an hour. I began to crave scripture. I had so much to learn and God was going to teach me. I would sit up late at night and pray, "Lord, You teach me what these scriptures mean for me, for my life, for my family. I want to hear what YOU have to say." Our merciful God began to open my eyes to many truths

I had missed along the way because I had never taken the time to learn them for myself.

My children were all under the age of 6, so I longed for their nap times. Quiet time was at a premium. I couldn't find it – I had to create it. It was then that I began scheduling my daily time with the Lord, searching my soul. I began Bible studies, prayer journaling, and reading the Word. As I began spending daily time with Him, His voice became clear and He began to use me in many ways.

I attended a Christian retreat in 2001 where I knew God was calling me to minister to women. God impressed upon my heart, "You have been so blessed, it is time you bless others." He later confirmed that calling through scriptures, friends and circumstances.

I was not immediately passionate about the calling. I didn't feel knowledgeable enough, or worthy enough for such a ministry. It wasn't until God revealed my life verse that I began to acknowledge my doubt as sin. The message version of Romans 12:1 reads, *"Take your everyday, ordinary life — your sleeping, eating, going-to-work, and walking around life — and place it before God as an offering."* I finally realized that God wants me, my whole being – my ordinary life.

The more I prayed the more doors God opened. I reluctantly walked through each door placed in my path, not feeling prepared or worthy of the opportunities. I began being asked to speak at conferences, lead Bible studies and mentor women. The leadership at our church asked me to lead our Women's

Ministry. I began writing weekly devotionals, which I still write today and send to women weekly around the world.

A couple of months before my husband was to retire from the military, he became involved in business with a man we later learned was a con-artist. God really began working on me. It was through the process of discovering the con-artist's unethical behavior, answering to the IRS, dealing with the FBI and attorneys that God began to strip away the outer layers of my hard heart. I quickly saw that so much of what I thought mattered – didn't. My perfect life was shattered, so I thought. God taught me again, He just wanted the real me. He needed me to be authentic and real to be able to relate to others.

I became very conscious of the fact that God could not truly use me if I was plastic and wearing a mask. God blessed my husband and me through that whole process and began to use me in ways I would have never imagined.

In 2006, I became very cognizant of my calling and purpose to connect women to God daily so that they too can live the life He has called them to. God began opening doors for speaking, teaching, writing and organizing women's conferences.

My passion today is to motivate and encourage women to draw near to the heart of God. Teaching others, through Bible studies that I've written, that their daily, personal time with God can be fun and exciting exhilarates me. I want women to know they are so special and worthy. God loves ordinary people, like me, because we relate to ordinary, everyday people. I love to teach—ordinary is amazing!

Alene Snodgrass

Fearfully and
Wonderfully Made

"I know, Lord, that the children you have given me are fearfully and wonderfully made. I praise you for these gifts; for I know full well that your works are wonderful. You reached into my womb and knitted a handsome young man, and a beautiful princess; you made them with your own hands. Lord, I am in awe of how you created them with such delicate and yet precise character. Aubrey is full of life and energy; she is feisty and strong willed; she has a motherly instinct, and is never short on compassion and empathy for others. Taylor is joyful, courageous, brave, and never meets a stranger. You created them with the very characteristics they would need to walk along the road of life you had so carefully planned."

In Oct. of 1999 Taylor was admitted to Driscoll Children's Hospital for what we thought was viral pneumonia. After a few nights in the hospital the doctors came in unexpectedly to announce that Taylor's heart was enlarging and that they felt he had developed a severe heart problem. That night nurses came to put in new IVs, interns came to listen to "the gallop", and doctors came to prepare us for a major procedure. God came to give us the gift of a pediatrician, Dr. Susan Shultez, a woman prepared to share His love as she prayed for Taylor's survival, and her colleagues' wisdom in performing a procedure on a heart much too weak to undergo the intensity of a heart cath. God was faithful to answer her prayers as promised in James 5:16, *"The prayer of a righteous man is powerful and effective."* She would become the instrument which God would use to build faith, hope, and joy despite a medical crisis. This would prove to be a life-changing experience for my family and me. This would be the experience that would show me just how fearfully and wonderfully we are made.

Taylor's heart had become too weak to care for the demands of his body. Outwardly he appeared healthy and full of life. Inwardly a struggle was occurring that was about to take his life and required an emergency heart transplant. On May 1, 2000, Taylor received his new heart. The five-hour surgery was beyond my comprehension as they explained how they had removed the heart and placed the new one in. I stared in amazement as they performed x-rays, and I could see each and every rib, the lungs, and that precious heart. The heart was pumping with such ease and in perfect time; it had so many valves and veins, and the chambers worked so well together. Taylor suddenly had pink cheeks and a radiance that could only come from a body so delicately made.

Upon this journey God engraved upon my heart many lessons seen through the eyes of my children, faithful friends and family, and through the example set by Dr. Shultez. She came into our life bearing witness to Matthew 6:8 *"Your Father knows what you need even before you ask."* She was an ordinary doctor who answered the call when it would have been easier to run to the next room. She gave of herself when things seemed in a state of confusion, and today she continues to allow God to use her as an instrument of healing, and teaches others about Christ's endless love in times of vulnerability. She has taught me how to live in God's time, not my time.

Aubrey's empathy for her brother led her to pray "God, thank you for helping Taylor breathe today." I quickly realized that life is about enjoying the simple, yet small, successes within a day. Her compassion often resulted in her taking Taylor's hand and walking down the halls and streets of Houston in silence. It was then that I realized that God takes our hand every day, often walking in silence, all the while ensuring comfort and love no matter where the road may lead. Today, Aubrey never misses an opportunity to kick around a soccer ball or laugh with her brother.

Taylor's bravery and courage saw him through endless blood draws and a major surgery. His trust in the doctors and nurses showed me the importance of walking in faith through all things. His humor and playful spirit gave us endless joy along a road that was often painful and weary. It was then that I saw that God can change what appears to be negative into something positive. Today, Taylor lives his life as God intended. His motto is "I have one life to live, and I am living it to the fullest." He never fears meeting his heavenly Father, and joins his sister in acknowledging the beauty of life, and embracing the love in each day.

I know, Lord, that the children you have given me are fearfully and wonderfully made.

Tamara Berry

Thy Will Be Done

For the majority of the fifty years I've lived on Earth, I have walked through life with a stride that is quick paced and one that is extremely focused in terms of my chosen path and the means to how and where I would arrive. However, I always seem to be in constant battle with an internal obstacle that never tires at planting seeds of doubt, despair and denial along the way. By the grace of God, my stride tends to place my steps ahead of this obstacle and typically I am successful at maneuvering out of its planned diversions and destructive intent.

Being raised Roman Catholic in a city with the honored name of Corpus Christi (Body of Christ), my four siblings and I were nurtured by loving parents and schooled in the Catholic Christian faith by a variety of dedicated stewards.

When I turned the age of twelve, the same age as that of young Taylor Berry, I too experienced heart disease, but not directly. My three older brothers were diagnosed with a rare heart abnormality called Idiopathic Hypertrophic Subaortic

Stenosis (IHSS). Though my younger sister and I did not have the disease, we were not immune to the emotional trauma and spiritual healing this trial would have on our family. Literally overnight these three young men, in their teens, began to encounter adult-sized emotions and decisions, under the care of our parents, which would leave indelible marks on many of the milestones throughout my life and the lives of others as well.

Though my life has been well-rooted in a Christian belief system, many times over I have hit what I felt was rock bottom. Each event or series of events would test my level of mental and spiritual maturity, or the lack thereof, would submit to the opposing force; the bottom made of rock, versus submitting to "The Rock" who has no bottom and who is, above all, God.

Throughout the Bible, God the Father has many endearing names; The Rock, Creator, Lord of Lords, King of Kings, Jesus, Savior, Friend, etc. In the book of Matthew and the book of Luke, our Friend and Savior, Jesus, tells us how to pray. In particular, He says; "Thy will be done". This portion of what is reverently referred to as "The Lord's Prayer" or "The Our Father" is a positive affirmation. A sublime and supreme promise, God's will, is going to take place; His will is going to happen: it shall be done. Jesus is telling us here that we must always have the mindset that what is coming; "Thy Kingdom", is true and definite. Jesus is telling us to continually transform our thoughts and our actions so that we can be found worthy to reside with Him in Heaven for eternity.

As mentioned above, when I was twelve, my three brothers were diagnosed with a rare heart disease. Over the course of the next thirty years, each would eventually die as a result of the disease. My eldest brother was the first to be diagnosed and he, at the young age of eighteen, had to immediately deal with his mortality straight on, due to the severity of his condition.

The night before my brother and our parents, left for Houston, Texas, where he would have open heart surgery, he sat with our family and slowly recited "The Our Father". My brother meticulously took each stanza and after saying it, he would, in his own words, tell us what Jesus' Word meant to him. I recall how he explained "Thy will be done" to us in a soft tone and with a slow delivery that, surprisingly, had a calming affect as we listened in awe. He spoke of God having planned things out in such a way that though we might not quite understand it now, we would really enjoy it later. He talked about how we as a family needed to not be let down by future events and despite the outcome of his surgery we must stay true to God and prepare ourselves so that we can be together forever in Heaven.

Roughly seventy-two hours after my brother concluded his rendition of "The Lord's Prayer", I found myself alone in the corner at a family friend's home where my younger sister and I were staying while our parents were away. I was praying as hard as I could and asking God to not take my brother. My brother had made it through surgery but his kidneys were not functioning well and he was now near death. Moments later, our friends rushed us to our home where our other two brothers were staying and we awaited "the call" from our Dad.

I hit rock bottom for the first time in my life when my third oldest brother handed me the phone. My world, where I was part of a well-rooted Christian family and where "all was well", was now upside down and sure to never correct itself, much less be the same again. Of course, our Mom and Dad continued to assure us that with God our family would make it through this and we would become stronger as a result. For me, I just kept remembering that twelve year-old boy afraid and alone in the corner of a small bathroom asking God, the Creator, to not let his big brother die.

"Thy will be done" is not a catch phrase, nor is it a short-lived resolution, a half baked attempt to make change in hopes to appease someone or something. It is a means to achieve an eternal end. I know, I just used an oxymoron – my apologies to all my English teachers throughout the years. "End" in this setting is meant as an objective. Though we are on this earth today, if we long to live eternally, we must remove our personal wants from the equation and rely on God's promise while we faithfully take action that mirrors His image and advocates our eternal end.

References to God's promise are mentioned throughout the Bible but one that speaks to me is from the book of James; "Blessed is a man who perseveres under trial; for once he has been approved, he will *receive the crown of life* which the Lord has promised to those who love Him."

To mirror His image, we need to have knowledge of Him. The truest resource of this knowledge is through "the Word" and is found, you got it, in the Bible. Whether you are driven to thumb through it, study it along with a structured guide, or read it cover to cover, the Bible is "the Word" and "the Word" is the truth and as written in the book of John, "… the truth shall set you free".

My childhood was packed full of knowledge that came from the Bible, but not so much from our family reading or studying it per se. Each day at St. Theresa Catholic parochial school, Sr. Claude and others would teach us kids' Bible-based curriculum, Baltimore Catechism at the time. My parents would pray the Rosary with us (each decade or mystery depicting blessed events found in the New Testament). I also participated in Christian-based activities in my youth; i.e., Ad Altare Dei n Scouting, Fellowship of Christian Athletes in High School, etc. These diverse and continuous sources of "the Word", and related knowledge remains an essential benchmark for me as I attempt to mirror God throughout my life.

Case in point: let's go back to my third-oldest brother handing me the phone and my Dad telling me what the glistening eyes of my two brothers had already communicated. To not have had a base load of religious knowledge, even at the age of twelve, could have proven devastating in years to come. Without knowing who God is, why Jesus died for us, what is expected in the Commandments and what "Thy Will Be Done" means, I might have never lifted myself from that rock bottom and resumed a life as God intended.

Yes, life is riddled with the occasional pitfall, yet we can live one filled with opportunities to add to our knowledge and understanding of the Word. We can choose to spend our lives trying to emulate Christ at and after each turn and to rid ourselves of selfish tendencies. If we choose to, we can surrender to God and live with the commitment that "Thy Will Be Done".

Ron Enderle

A Prayer Answered

Several years ago, we purchased a Kayak at a sporting goods store in Houston. Given the vehicle that we were driving, we did not have a way to transport it back to Corpus Christi. My wife said, "Don't worry; I will pick it up when I come back to Houston in a couple of weeks. They can tie it down on top of our Jeep."

When the day came that my wife was to drive to Houston, I was concerned that she would have to deal with a kayak strapped to the top of our vehicle. Late on the morning of her return, we talked as she was on her way to the sporting goods store.

I kept thinking about my wife and I felt an overwhelming need to pray for her. While I have experienced the need to pray at various times in my life, this urging was very different. It was as if I were being pulled to pray without delay. Around 2:30 in the afternoon, I went into my office and closed the door. I spent a few minutes in prayer, asking that my wife be protected and that she have a safe trip home. Shortly after my prayer, I called her to see how things were going. Immediately after she answered the phone, I could tell that something was wrong. She was out of breath and her voice was shaky. There was hesitation as she explained that she must have fallen asleep while driving. She said that she was in the middle of heavy traffic on the freeway and that the next thing she knew, she awakened as she was driving on grass, headed towards the feeder road. She said that she was alright, but was shaken by what had happened. She told me that she had driven up to an abandoned service station and that she was going to try to get some rest. She told me that she would call me back.

After about an hour, she called me and explained that she had been in the middle lane of a freeway and there was traffic on all sides. The strap that was used to tie down the front-end of the kayak had mesmerized her as it flapped in the wind. She said that she does not know how it was possible that she crossed the lanes without being hit by another vehicle.

Without a doubt, the power of prayer kept her safe. There was a reason that I felt compelled to prayer at that very moment.

Jose Moncada

A Fisher of Men

When I was twelve my father, a battalion commander in the US Army, was stationed in Hawaii. To me, a young man very interested in surfing, it was a dream come true. I started surfing the day we arrived in Hawaii and quickly excelled. By fourteen I was surfing the North Shore competitively. Life was as good as it gets. I was winning contests, there was surfing, there were parties, and lots of pretty women. Then it happened: my great dad, my idol, got notice he was deploying to Vietnam at the height of the war. We were to stay in Hawaii while he was gone. I remember him pulling me aside and telling me that while he was gone, I would be the man of the house, and it would be my job to take care of my mother, brother and sister. I didn't realize it then, but he didn't mean it literally; he was just trying to make me feel important. I didn't know then that those words would remain with me a large part of my adolescence and adult life.

I quickly found out that at fourteen years of age I was not equipped. At night when everyone was in bed

I used to lie in bed and listen to my mother crying. She was heartbroken and filled with fear that my father could be killed at anytime. I couldn't cope, and turned to the things that made me feel better; surfing and parties. Soon I began to stay away from home, where my family needed me, and I am still ashamed of that choice to this day. To help with the loneliness, I turned to drugs. Hawaii had all the party favors one could want: pot laced with heroin, the best opium, hash and LSD. The more I used the drugs the less I felt. It all came to a head when after a surfing contest a friend and I celebrated our success with some pot laced with heroin and malt liquor and shortly thereafter were involved in an automobile accident that led to a one-year stint in the hospital. I was lucky to be alive but mother said luck had nothing to do with it; God saved me. She had always told me God had work for me to do.

My family moved back to the mainland, but I had to stay in Hawaii because I couldn't be moved until I got out of traction. To cope once again, I chose drugs. You would think it hard to use illegal drugs in a military hospital but I found a way. The drugs dulled the pain, but little by little they changed me. My hurtful ways were directed mostly at my family. When I was able to go back home to my family, life was awful, and my father kicked me out of the house at fifteen. I relied on shoplifting and petty thefts to eat and support my habits.

I had always believed Jesus was my Savior but was not ready at this point to listen to His plan for me. God continued to let me run my own course and finally, after being arrested for theft, the authorities sent me back to my parents' custody. My drug use continued, but I managed to graduate from high school and go on to get a college degree, a master's in finance, and find a good job. Life continued to be a party as I worked days and afterwards would head straight for the bars, only to leave and find my dealer to "kick it up a notch" with some coke. It didn't take long before my job performance suffered. Even though I made good money I owed money to everyone; bar tabs, coke dealers, car notes and friends. I left my job and drifted around a while. Still not convinced that my bad habits were affecting my life, I became more depressed and the partying didn't seem to cover the pain and loneliness I was feeling.

Then I met my wife, and things began to change. I wanted a life with her, and one day I knelt down and pleaded with God to help me in my life. My relationship with God started that day. Things were hard at first; I had a lot of baggage from my irresponsible behavior, but none of that mattered because we were happy and were rebuilding our lives spiritually.

God has used my past and my failures to help others with their broken lives. I became a disciple for the Lord. God had been there all along. He let me make my mistakes, mistakes that almost killed me several times, and when I was ready to accept His invitation and make Him Lord of my life He brought the best out of David Smith.

I wake up everyday and have this great desire to spread the word of what God has done in my life to encourage others to find true happiness in a relationship with God. He made me want to be a "fisher of men", a disciple.

Are you ready to be blessed? If you are; say yes to a life with Jesus, say yes to that relationship that God wants with you. God takes you where you are in life. He has forgiven you and me for all our sins. God's amazing grace, how sweet the sound!

The Lord took me, the drug taking, selfish, thieving, wretch that I was, and made me a fisher of men, a disciple. I am proof positive that God will lead you, whatever your past. All you have to do is say, "Yes Lord", and He will do the rest.

David Smith

A Great God

I was raised "barely" in the church. By that I mean we went occasionally. My parents were both deaf and would say that they had no idea what they were talking about in church. They believed in God, though, and so did I.

It wasn't until I had my children that I gave it much thought. Then I gave it a lot of thought. Having a child is such a miracle that you can't help to think about God's greatness for such a blessing to be growing inside of you.

My kids were baptized and we went to church regularly. But it wasn't until my life stared to spiral out of control with a husband who was an alcoholic and drug addict that I found myself really praying and listening for God's wisdom.

In the back of my mind I knew my brother would be there to help me with the kids, but suddenly he was diagnosed with a brain tumor and there was just him and me here for family. I took on all of his medical issues on top of being the only support for my family and having two babies. This made things even worse as my husband felt I was "choosing" my brother over him, which caused his problems to get much worse. Then I was diagnosed with breast cancer and at the same time was going through a divorce. I was scared. No matter what, I had always been able to count on myself and now I didn't know if I could do that. Who would take care of us? What would happen to my babies if I died?

Somehow with what should have been my darkest moment in my life, there was light. I had to learn to trust God. As a take-charge kind of person, this was very hard, but amazingly, as I learned this, my life seemed to turn around.

I am a truly blessed person. I have a wonderful husband today, two great kids who have had to learn how to handle adversity, a great home, a great job, a great church, but most importantly a GREAT GOD from who all blessings flow.

Jo-Anne Lamorey

My Testimony ~ 2009

A few years ago I realized I did not have the answers I thought I had or could count on. Despite being raised as a Protestant Christian all my life (my dad was an elder in both churches we attended during my childhood), I didn't grow up in a gentle home … but one that was fairly judgmental, critical and aggressively opinionated. We did not *ever* read the Bibles we each had.

I was involved in Young Life, VBS, Sunday school and Christian camps as a kid. As a senior in college and during my Master's Degree, I re-discovered a childhood minister and attended services during those years as well.

After college, I still considered myself a Christian, but did not attend church or read the Bible. I married a non-practicing Catholic who was probably (although not publicly) agnostic, and we divorced six years later.

After meeting Curt, we attended the church I had joined earlier and were later married there. After our daughter was born, we moved to the Dallas area and joined the same type of church of my youth ... attending and serving with the same enthusiasm. Even Bible study and Habitat for Humanity did not awaken our spiritual numbness.

Several years ago our daughter was invited to Crossroad Bible Church's ("CBC") VBS and Half Time programs, and one Sunday we decided the irritating traffic hold-up here might actually be God asking us to slow down and come in, so we did.

Although still not as often as I should, I have been reading God's word *more than ever in my life* since we came to CBC, and I realize for the first time, I <u>need</u> to be around mature Christians. *"Brothers and Sisters in Christ"* had very little meaning before it dawned on me what an incredible gift it is to be considered a child of the Most High God; family of an all powerful Father. My cavalier attitude toward being a member in the Kingdom of God seems [to me now] so brain dead, so stone-hearted, and I am at times in awe of teens and young adults who already "get it" — when it's taken me more than half my life.

In these past years, I have changed. I've learned to feel God's presence in my life, to realize that He's always been there, and to feel the <u>need</u> to stay close to Him both in prayer and by letting Him unravel the mysteries He's saved for me if I'll follow Him. Striving *daily* to ask for forgiveness and knowing He forgives me is both humbling, and for me, revealing of just how sinful I *continually* am.

I have quit feeling uncool, unintelligent and embarrassed regarding my devotion to Christ. Not because it came to me of my own accord, but because God put directly in my path men and women I respect and more importantly, who love and respect Him... to show me the way. He also allowed life's scarring moments to drop me to my knees a few times.

What other god of this world ever loved His people so much that He offered them His only Son so that one day we, too, would also escape a "forever death" ...and then waited patiently for these earthly children to realize what this meant for them? I must say now ... after too many years of lukewarm faith, that my finest blessing is that He knocked once again at my door, and finally, FINALLY I opened it, accepted His gift ...and invited Him in.

Sherri Sund

Grace

The other day I was in HEB doing my weekly shopping when I saw a friend who had recently invited us to a lovely party in her home the month before. I had RSVP'd on the card "Yes! With bells on!" But, the evening of the party, one thing after another happened – a late husband, a teen crisis, and an unexpected out-of-town guest dropped in for a visit. My husband looked at me and said, "I just don't know how we can get in our dress clothes and get there before the party is over." I felt guilty and regretful, but went on to bed. So, when I saw the hostess looking through the canned vegetables, I ducked behind the end of the aisle to hide. I just could not face her.

The disciple Peter had reason to feel shame, regret, and guilt. We know from the Gospel that Peter denies Jesus, not once, not twice, but three times! He was asked two times if he was one of Jesus' disciples and he answered "I AM NOT!" (YES! WITH BELLS ON!). And then he was asked if he was with Jesus in the olive garden, and he said "I was not."

Then, as Jesus said it would, the rooster crowed. And in Luke it says when the rooster crowed, Jesus and Peter had eye contact. How horrible Peter must have felt. But he did not duck down and hide. Peter could have gone away in shame. He could have taken that failure and let it rule his life. Peter could have gone the way of Judas, by going away from God in shame and guilt and taking his life.

But instead Peter took that moment of failure and turned it into a moment of decision. He went towards God, not away from Him. He went on to Jerusalem and stood before thousands and talked boldly about Jesus Christ. This is such an example to me, because when I make a bad decision or knowingly make a mistake, I want to hide, to turn out the lights, to get under the covers and not show my face to anyone, much less God. But God has a way of shining His light on us. In Him there is no darkness at all. So we face the 'SON' and turn our face to him and draw nearer. And he may discipline us, but eventually he gives us undeserved grace, a gift that can only be given by Him.

So, fast-forward to a Friday morning after the resurrection. By this time, Jesus had already shown himself to the disciples three times. But this morning, they had been fishing all night and were tired and frustrated, as they had not caught many fish. Their livelihoods depended on fishing, so when Jesus called out to them from the shore to cast their nets to the other side, they were dubious. They did not recognize him, and wondered what he was talking about. All of a sudden, John says to Peter, "That's Jesus!" and Peter jumps out of the boat and swims as fast as possible to his Lord. He did not hide from Jesus; on the contrary, he wanted to get to him as fast as he could. It was as if he could not wait another second.

If there is something like a sin, a mistake, or a grudge, that is keeping you apart from Jesus, recognize it, get into conversation with God about it and abandon it. Jesus Christ not only embraced Peter – a man who had denied Him three times – he gave him a promotion and told him, "Peter, I want you to tend my sheep." He not only gave him mercy, he gave him GRACE. So when you mess up, confess, be honest, and lean into the Lord. He will reward you in ways you cannot even imagine. 1 John 1:9 says, *"If we confess our sins, he is faithful and just and will forgive us our sins."*

After ducking around the aisles in HEB like a Judas, I went home, wrote my friend an honest note and told her I was sorry. I saw her the other day, and in her most gracious way, she gave me a hug and a big smile. Imagine that!

Barbara Hawes Morris

No Deals Just Promises

It was the night of December 13, 1997 when my life as I knew it would change forever. My fiancée and I had been dating for 11 months and were SO happy. Everything was perfect! We were celebrating at his business' annual Christmas party, having a fabulous time. He was introducing me to all of his friends, I was getting to know his family, and life was really wonderful. It was time to call it a night. We drove to his home for a late dinner in separate cars. It was my turn to stop and pick up the burgers. I arrived to his home first but he wasn't there.

Something wasn't right. I knew immediately what had happened. I got back in my car and re-traced the route I thought he had taken, feeling the dread the whole way…and then I saw it…the sirens, the police cars, the overturned SUV lying in the ditch. Just beyond that I saw Doug, lying face down, and so still.

Somehow he lost control of the vehicle, running off the road, overcorrecting and ultimately flipping his Ford Explorer. He was ejected from the car, sustaining massive head injuries. I remember falling to my knees in the parking lot of Memorial Hospital's Emergency Room, clutching my silver cross necklace I was wearing and "making deals" with God. I promised everything I could think of, I remember telling him I would follow Him for the rest of my days if He would only let the love of my life live.

Doug was pronounced dead the following day.

I lost someone very dear to me that day… And in the days to follow, I learned that God doesn't make deals… He makes promises. He promises to love us, to guide us, and to strengthen us.

After sleeping for days, losing 15 pounds and living in a grief-stricken fog for 2 weeks, it was Christmas. I lay in bed that night and waited until midnight so I could wish Jesus a happy birthday and **PRAY** for strength, strength just to brush my hair, strength to nourish my body, strength to live. On Christmas morning I woke up and breathed in new life. He gave me the strength that day to get up and face life again; I was bruised, but not broken. He is the one who took care of me…he brought me back to life.

Thank you God for Your amazing grace.

Lisa Hensley

Before and After God's Redeeming Grace

I have seen the ugliest of ugly in my life. I have lived the life of an addict.... crystal methamphetamines to be exact. That is a type of speed. It comes in the form of a rock or powder that you can "shoot up" or snort or smoke.

It's taking the world over in so many ways. I have seen many lives and families torn apart because of this addictive drug. It does not discriminate. It can destroy rich, poor, students, moms, dads, professionals, pastor's kids, doctors, lawyers, anyone. The devil is right in the middle of this drug. I lived in Arizona where the drug is rampant.

I was so addicted that it took over my life. It started out as social interaction at parties, and then it became the worst lie I have ever seen or experienced. It destroyed my life and my family's lives. I became homeless, with nowhere to go and nowhere to turn. I was constantly looking for the next line to snort or bowl to smoke. At 5'9" and weighing about 106 lbs.,

I was desperate, hopeless, and in denial. My teeth were severely decayed and a couple of them were missing.

When you're in the throes of a crystal meth addiction, you don't eat; the roots of your teeth are affected, and everything in your life is centered around getting high. There is a euphoric feeling as if you can conquer anything... but that is the big lie! All of your money is going to the drug. Bills don't get paid, food doesn't get bought, and you isolate yourself from your family and anyone not using.

My mom found out what condition I was in and sent me a plane ticket to come home. I did, reluctantly leaving my 7-year-old son at the airport with his dad. That was in 1994. I was worn out, hopeless and empty. I was emaciated and looked like a toothless rat. All along my mom had been on her knees praying God would deliver me and bring me to my knees at the foot of our awesome savior, Jesus Christ.

> 1st Peter 5:8 says, *"Be self-controlled and alert. Your enemy, the devil, prowls around like a roaring lion looking for someone to devour. Resist him, standing firm in the faith, because you know that your brothers throughout the world are undergoing the same kind of suffering."*

O.K. How did I still have hope?

I accepted Christ as my savior when I was 7 years old. I remember the exact moment that I felt His

Holy Spirit reveal the truth to me of what Jesus had done for me and the entire human race. I know that His suffering was greater than I could comprehend, and that He did rise from the dead! I was sold out to Christ. I realized that we all get distracted and that we all fall short of the glory of God, but He died and rose again so we could be redeemed and forgiven and not have to carry around those pains, burdens, guilt, and shame.

1 Peter 5:10 says, *"And the God of all grace, who called you to His eternal glory in Christ after you have suffered a little while, will Himself restore you and make you strong, firm and steadfast. To Him be the power for ever and ever."*

When I came back to Corpus in February of 1994, I was broken and just a shell of a woman. When I got off of the airplane, my mom and step-dad were waiting for me. The look on their faces was of sheer shock. They were heartbroken that I had done this to myself and my life.

Matthew 11:28 Jesus tells us, *"Come to me all you who are weary and burdened and I will give you rest."* My mom nurtured me, loved me and prayed me back to life. I slept and ate and slept some more for about 3 weeks. Then we started exercising and walking together, and my Mom knew it was time for me to start my walk back to Christ. She told me about a church that had a contemporary service, which was something I had never experienced before. I found that I was drawn to the music. It felt so anointed, so holy...

Have you ever heard a song and it just drew you into the presence of our Almighty God? That's what happens for me when I entered His throne room... I started to feel human again, except this time I felt renewed and I knew God had called me back home! I started to read the scriptures and they spoke to me personally. It was God teaching me and making me new again! His living word breathed life back into my heart and soul. Little by little I started making goals for myself, and God helped me complete each one! He brought the scripture Matthew 7:7 to my attention and it was just what I needed to hear:

"Ask and it will be given to you, seek and you will find, knock and the door will be opened. For everyone who ask will receive, he who seeks finds, and to him who knocks, the door will be opened!" It opened my eyes to see His promises were meant for me and you.

What I've learned is that God wants the best for us, no matter what we've done. He loves us so much, that he came so that we may have everlasting life and live it abundantly! He forgives us and loves us right where we are. God has chosen special gifts for each one of us to use, to bring people closer to Him and to each other.

1 Peter 4:10-*11* *"Each one should use what-ever gift he has received to serve others, faith-fully administering God's grace in its various forms. If anyone speaks, he should do it as*

one speaking the very words of God. If anyone serves, he should do it with the strength God provides, so that in all things God may be praised through Jesus Christ. To Him be the glory and power for ever and ever."

When I look at my "BEFORE AND AFTER" pictures, I think back on my experiences and see God in all of them, over and over again, no matter how much of a mess I was. It's hard for me to look back at those, but I can end that memory with a smile and gratefulness for God's AMAZING GRACE. (My life really is like a song!)

Psalm 37:3-4 *"Trust in the Lord and do good; dwell in the land and enjoy safe pasture. Delight yourself in the Lord and He will give you the desires of your heart."*

God has given me the desires of my heart. He instilled in me the desire to glorify Him and teach others through song. Never in a million years would I have believed that His plan for me would lead me to where I am now. I have been the praise leader at St. John's UMC Contemporary "Crossroads" service for 11 years. He has allowed me to minister to people of all ages through conferences, concerts, retreats, mission trips, and Walks to Emmaus. My band, Prophecy, and I, have opened for Building 429 and Michael W. Smith, popular contemporary Christian performers. I have even had the honor of singing for Governor Rick Perry of Texas.

I've truly seen God's glorious redeeming grace through the eyes of an addict, the homeless, the lost, and lonely. This experience led me to write the chorus of Prophecy's first single "Here I Am"...

'Somebody's sayin' I'll find my way home,
Somebody's cryin' I don't wanna be alone.
Reach out your hands and touch somebody's
Life.
There's a lot of people out there, who
Can't get it right."

Romans 15:13 says, *"May the God of hope fill you with all the joy and peace as you trust in Him so that you may overflow with hope by the power of the Holy Spirit.*

Debra Scott-Brown

The Sum of Stuff

The whirlwind is beginning to subside. We are over the shock of loss, and it may take us some time to loosen the paranoia from our thinking—we see fire hazards everywhere, and frankly one could go nuts trying to make his house completely fireproof. Because of the conditions of drought and high winds on February 28, only a stone house with a metal roof would have survived, but that would not have protected its contents. The intense heat would have ignited the contents inside. The firemen who were on the hill when the fireball rolled up the bluff said they had to flee for their lives when it arrived.

God has been blessing us so much I'm about to bust. I don't know why He has graced us so, and I am struggling with unfounded guilt for being lavished with so much when others seem to be experiencing more need and loss. Since the very beginning, every one of our needs has been met, and in many ways miraculously. Three friends "happened" to be on the east side of Bastrop before the fire reached us. They had ample time to flee the exceedingly long diversion before Highway 71 was closed. Instead, they risked their lives to come to our aid, not knowing where the front of the fire was at the time. If they had not arrived and helped us pack up our cars and truck, much more would have been lost. We would have had to leave one of our vehicles.

Neighbor Patsy captured on her camera the explosion of my shop at the edge of the bluff as she and Joe fled the bluff behind us. Her digital camera recorded that picture at 3:33 P.M. We had left our driveway a little before 3:30. As we were leaving, I called my friend Richard in a nearby town, telling him we were coming to stay the night at his house. First, I figured we would be returning to an unscathed house the next day, but secondly, Richard's that kind of friend: The last thing I saw, leaving the bluff, was the billowing smoke growing larger from each gust from the sustained 40 mph wind. Glancing at the towering smoke in the direction of the bluff as we drove toward Rosanky, I concluded that our house was gone. It was then I prayed, "Lord, if our house is gone, please give us the strength in the days to come to demonstrate your grace and faithfulness." My wife Adella told me later that about that time, a pastor friend was praying with her on her cell phone.

After spending a restless night in a strange bed, we got up after hearing Richard wander around in the kitchen. He is a noisy wanderer, and his coffee was bitter that day, but not as much as the news he had to deliver. As a hint of dawn was breaking, I mentioned to Richard that I needed to call my neighbor Joe for news on the condition of our house.

"You don't need to. He called me," Richard injected.

"He did? When?"

"About three this morning. It's bad."

"I'm not surprised," I said after sighing and swallowing what felt like the spoon from my last bite of oatmeal. And I wasn't surprised, though throughout the night I had wishful thoughts that the fire had skipped over our house, visions as it were of only charred leaves around our home.

The night was slowly yielding to dawn as Richard and Ladelle drove us east on Highway 71, but its faintness could only expose the silhouette of both charred and untouched trees, unable to reveal the path the fire had taken the day before.

Up the hill to our property lay the blackened ground where the wildfire had passed. It was not until Richard cut the engine that we realized exactly how bad it was. Mingled in car-light and dawn our house appeared to be just a thick blanket of snow in which the only things standing were the piers, encircled by flat sheets of ice. What once was a carport now resembled metal moth wings. Like mixed metaphors, feelings of confusion and loss mingled with the inescapable fact that nothing in this world is permanent; nothing is truly ours to keep. That is the sum of *stuff*—in the end, everything is ashes.

If it can be said without sounding absurd, I believe the loss of our house presents our kids the freedom to treat their inheritance with prudence. Since its construction, they had insisted they would never sell the house, even if their absence in the area would create some hardships. Now, they should not feel obligated to hold on to what we made.

But they, too, shared in our grief. Sunday afternoon Jeremy and Liz were with us sifting through the rubble looking for evidence of things we held dear. There were tears for their mother as she held the broken tea pot given to her by Grandmother decades ago, and hugs were plentiful, but their hearts ached more for fear this loss meant more to us than it did.

God works good in all things for those who love the Lord, to those who are called according to His purpose. I believe that if there is anything to the rain falling on the just and the unjust, there must be good that God works in all things for those who do not love the Lord as well. And I have an idea that the difference between those who love and don't is those who are called according to his purpose see the good and those who aren't don't want to.

So, this is what I see.

Before the last stick of furniture was consumed, friends and neighbors were praying for us. When news confirming the loss was shared, we received calls and emails from people everywhere—each echoing the same: "What can I do?"

Our hearts are touched by the giving people have demonstrated from every direction from friend and stranger alike, near and far. What was most meaningful, behind every gift of money, clothes, gift cards, offers of shelter indefinitely, borrowed furniture—all within the realm of stuff—were the sympathetic tears and promised thoughts and prayers from calls, visits, and cards.

We have always enjoyed being givers. We are not accustomed to being full-time receivers. This is a new role for us. We are thankful for all that has been done for us. And we pray that we will be sensitive to God's leadership in each decision we need to make.

Larry Smith

Total Security

Ever since I can remember, my parents took me to church with them. I attended Sunday School and church every week, but it wasn't a personal experience. However, early in my life I came to know Jesus as my personal Savior. On a retreat in Vicksburg, MS, I accepted Christ. I was in the seventh grade.

He's been my Savior, my friend....I've grown in Him, studied His Word, AND walked away from Him. I've lived in the far country and then come home to Him. Over time, He revealed so many wounds in my heart and soul, some of which I thought would always be a part of me and my personality. It's only in the last several years of my life that I have sought His healing and let him truly heal me.

I finally let Him under my skin of insecurity …. I've been insecure ALL of my life...I've never thought that I've been pretty enough, smart enough, or talented enough. I've never won any awards, wasn't the high school or college girl to date. I always looked at myself and thought, "Oh, I just wish that I was smarter, more talented, prettier, or just more of everything".

This bond of insecurity had truly become an outer garment of mine. I often wore it proudly. I hid behind it. My insecurity allowed me a way to say no to opportunities, such as, "I can't, I'm not talented, I don't have those gifts, I'm too scared to try, and I don't really have anything to offer". It was an obstacle of grace for me....an obstruction that prevented me from God's plan **for** me. God could not reach me through this skin of mine. Through Christ and a dear Christian sister, on an Emmaus Walk, I let Christ take off this outer skin and heal me. Now, don't be confused, I'm still unsure of myself and doubt myself but God has done a work in me.

Never have I been so touched by realizing those words from a children's book....Love You Forever by Robert Munsch. I had known for years that God loved me but I had NEVER accepted that He liked me.

I'm still learning every day that my TOTAL security comes from my relationship with Christ. As I surrender myself to Him and accept His Spirit within me, I'm healed and I'm His. Remember, Isaiah 49:16, "See, I have inscribed you on the palms of my hands", and Jeremiah 1:5, "Before I formed you in the womb I knew you, and before you were born I claimed you".

Praise the Lord Jesus; He is my Redeemer, my Savior, my Alpha and Omega.

Kathy Hayes

*My heart is overflowing with a good theme;
I create my composition concerning the
King.
My tongue is the pen of a ready writer.
Psalm 45:1*

*In the beginning God created the heavens
and the earth. The earth was without form,
and void: and darkness was on the face of
the deep. And the Spirit of God was hovering
over the face of the waters. Then God said,
"Let there be light", and there was light.*
Genesis 1:1-3

He has continued to create, mold, fashion, and change things, the Spirit ever hovering over, waiting, watching, guiding, giving, continuing from the beginning of time to this day, to give 'Light' to all who want to escape the darkness.

The creation account is the story of my life. Before I gave my life to Christ I had no purpose, no hope; my life was empty, completely void, and darkness filled the deepest parts of me. Yet, the Spirit of God was hovering over me, waiting, watching, patient, until just the right moment when I would let Him speak to me. When I was ready to come out of the pit of despair and utter darkness, when I cried out to God, then He moved from hovering over me into action. He immediately responded to my cry, for that is what He had been waiting for all along. His response was "Let there be light" in her life, and there was light.

One of my favorite stories in the Bible is in Luke 8:26-39. In this story a man lived for years in dark tombs, among the dead, completely controlled by Satan. My life before Christ paralleled the life of this man. The compassion of Jesus flowed out and covered him. Jesus changed his heart, healed him and released him from Satan's captivity. In response, the man wanted nothing more than to sit at the feet of Jesus in worship. Yet, surprisingly, Jesus said no. He had a plan for this man. He told the man to go back home to his family and friends and tell them how Jesus had changed his life.

Once I was lost, living in darkness among the spiritually dead, and enslaved by Satan, until I met Jesus. He came to me, saw my need, felt compassion for me, healed me, forgave me, and changed me. I want to stay sitting at the feet of Jesus yet He tells me, "No. I need you to go and tell everyone what I have done for you."

When Christ revealed Himself to me I was at a point in my life where I truly felt I had no hope. I was miserable, lost and very much alone. No one knew how I felt and the things of my past haunted me. I knew I needed the Lord's help if I was going to go on so I gave my life to Jesus, but I didn't know what to do next. I was attending church but I didn't know God intimately. I just sat in His house on Sundays. I knew a lot of the people there prayed and read the Bible everyday so that's where I began. I found this to be the key to knowing God. It's called a relationship. Through studying His word and talking to Him on a daily basis I began to understand not only who He is and how much He loves me, but also who He wants me to be. He has a plan for my life and I didn't realize that before. Not just any plan. The Bible says it's a good plan. (Jeremiah 29:11)

He changed my heart. With that came the realization that my life is really not my life at all. It is His life lived out through me. It's not about me. It's all about Him. He is in complete control of every situation. He created this awesome world with all its beauty, perfect in every way, until sin messed it up. Then God stepped in and through His Son, made the way to save us from that sin. He always has a plan to make things right. He's with me through every trial, temptation, and fear. He shares my joys and catches my tears. He understands when I make a mistake, always forgives, and shows me a lesson to be learned. He listens to my problems and helps me solve them. His plan is to use my life to glorify Him. He has a message to tell to all nations and He has chosen me as one of His messengers, just as he chose the man who lived in the tombs. There is nothing more humbling than this. There is no other thought more overwhelming than to know that the Almighty, Creator of the universe, has chosen me to help Him fulfill His plan.

In the whole scheme of things, I am nothing. When I consider the world, the universe, the galaxies, infinite beyond our wildest imagination, I am less than a speck of dust, nothing. He is everything. He took nothing and created everything. If He can do that with nothing, the possibilities of what He has in store for you and me are unfathomable.

My past is history. My life, my future, is HIS story. Wouldn't you like to be a part of His story as well? I gave my life to Christ and I have no regrets. It's not an easy road to walk, but He never leaves my side. I pray that if you are reading this and you do not have a personal relationship with Jesus, that today will be the day you let go of your life and turn it over to Him. Let Him do with your life what He has done with mine. He took nothing, and created, changed, and saved me from darkness by giving me the light of the Son, His Son.

Then Jesus spoke to them again, saying, *"I am the light of the world. He who follows Me shall not walk in darkness, but have the light of life."* John 8:12

Sheri C.

Are you ready to go
to sleep tonight?

Although both my mom and dad went to church as teenagers, I did not grow up going to church. I knew about God, but that was about it. In sixth grade my friend invited me to go on a church Beach Retreat to South Padre Island. It just sounded like a fun week at the beach to me. As much as I resisted, the Lord softened my heart each day during that week. On the last night, I found myself asking the Lord into my life and heart. The next week, I was baptized for the first time in the Sanctuary of that church, Second Baptist Church (SBC) in Houston, Texas. I continued to go to church and Bible study with my friend and her parents throughout the rest of junior high school.

I seemed to have it all in high school, cheerleader, class president, homecoming court, boyfriends, honor student…Why did I need God? I didn't go to church at all. I can't even remember missing it or thinking about it. This was a time for me, and I was doing just fine without God.

I even went to "Baptist" Baylor University for 4 years of undergraduate and 2 years of graduate school and managed to do it without setting foot into church all 6 years. I still didn't need God.

After leaving the "Baylor Bubble" I moved back to Houston to work. Something felt missing in my life. On the outside all looked well...I had an MBA, a great job and new car...still something was missing. I felt led to go back to Second Baptist Church. I didn't know anyone there anymore and it was even bigger now...I knew I wanted to check it out again, but I was afraid.

On a September day in 1997, I went back to SBC, walked down the isle to make a public recommitment and decided to go to a Bible study class. Since I didn't know a soul, I scanned the list of classes and stopped when I saw the name of a class teacher that was a counselor at the beach retreats I attended in junior high...that seemed like exactly where I should be. At first I only attended Bible study each Sunday. I was easing into this "God thing" slowly and really was in it for the fellowship mostly.

In March of 1998, my aunt Peggy and my cousin Terri had just gone on a spiritual retreat called the 'Walk to Emmaus' and they urged my mom and me to go. We were hesitant, but willing. This was the jumpstart I needed for growing in my spiritual walk. The week of the Emmaus Walk was an eye-opening experience to me. I started realizing that I was really missing out on something by not going to church services each week. I really began to fully accept Christ into my heart. I started getting involved...in my church in Bible study class leadership, organizing socials, joining and leading small groups, reading the Bible daily, teaching Bible study classes and even becoming a High School beach retreat counselor.

Another blessing happened in January of 2000 when my parents joined SBC and started going to church with me, joined a Bible study class, signed up for couples small groups, even quickly became secretaries of their class. I enjoyed so much going to church with my parents...this was new since again it was not customary growing up. I am also an only child and very close with my parents. It gave me great joy to see my parents growing in relationship with the Lord since it had also become so important to me.

In the summer of 2000, I was fortunate enough to be able to take a journey to Israel with about 8 girls from my church. God worked on me full-force and that experience changed me forever! I renewed my dedication to Christ by being re-baptized in the Jordan River on Fathers' Day 2000. I was so blessed that I could share that experience with some close girlfriends. This was a new beginning in my spiritual journey. That Christmas I made copies of my Israel Journal for my family and close friends – that was my first small attempt to directly witness to my loved ones.

My job took me out of town to San Francisco, California every week (Monday – Thursday) for almost the entire year of 2001. I felt like my job situation kept me from growing with the Lord because I couldn't sign up for a small group in Houston...but finally I realized that God was in California too!!! While in California that week, the Lord placed about 8 Christian colleagues in my life. I began going to BSF (Bible Study Fellowship) every Monday night; I started a Beth Moore Bible Study with a couple of women every Tuesday night and attended a contemporary praise and worship service on Wednesday nights. Every night of my week in California was booked...then Sunday's were for SBC!

During this time, my parents and I became focused on the Lord in every way. We talked about God, read the Bible together, prayed and even sang hymns together. We had an overwhelming desire to witness to our family through our changed lives and a deep concern for the salvation of our loved ones. My dad beamed with joy when he told me that the SBC had asked him to serve as a deacon. He said he felt unworthy (don't we all), but he was honored to further serve his church that had given him back his faith and relationship with Jesus. He was ordained on November 7, 2001.

Sunday, December 2, 2001, I finished my Christmas cards and Christmas letter. I had spoken to my Dad that night and told him I needed to run out and by stamps so I could mail my cards before I left again for California the next morning. He begged me not to leave the house for stamps since it was already dark outside. I told him I wouldn't. He was always trying to protect me from the world and ensure my safety! When I hung up the phone, I realized that it was only 6:00pm. I knew that I couldn't make a practice of only stepping foot outside my house during daylight hours - So I disobeyed my Dad and bought stamps and mailed out my Christmas cards and letter!!

On Thursday, December 6, 2001, while sleeping in my bed in California, I awoke to frightening call. It took me about five minutes to realize that the hysterical lady on the other end of the line was my mom and another minute or two to understand the words she was uttering… "I think Daddy is dead". I think I was in shock until about an hour later when the doctor's finally confirmed our worst nightmare. I called the emergency room to get an update and our dear friend Mark Ramsey said to me "Kristina, your Father has gone to be with the Lord". I fell to the floor sobbing and crying out to the Lord. I immediately thanked God that a large group of mom's Sunday School class had gotten to the hospital to be with mom so she wouldn't be alone anymore.

Now…I couldn't get home! I'd missed the red-eye flight out that morning. I felt so alone and I just prayed to God to be with me on the drive to the airport in the rain and fog, that long 3.5 hour flight and the ride out to Mom's. As I continued to pray in the San Francisco airport, I heard my name. It was my good friend Jamia Cotten from SBC in Houston. Jamia was in San Francisco for work that week and was on my flight. God had us assigned in seats 4A and 4B. We couldn't believe our eyes! I knew it was God that put her on my flight with me and sitting right next to me. God heard my cry — I was not alone. About 12 hours after hearing the news, I was finally at my mother's side.

That first year was hard...The stress of trying to help my mom figure out and close out my Dad's business, dissolving of business partnerships, the sale of cars and their home, and the purchase of a new home while dealing with our grief was overwhelming. But I felt the power of prayer. I experienced the love of a church family who picked us up and carried us when we couldn't walk ourselves. I have been sustained by the Holy Spirit and the Holy Spirit prayed for me when I didn't know what to pray. Romans 8:26 says, *"Likewise the Spirit helps us in our weakness; for we do not know how to pray as we ought, but the Spirit himself intercedes for us with sighs too deep for words."*

God has given me peace, strength, wisdom and discernment – just enough for each day! Philippians 4:5-7 says *"Let your gentleness be evident to all. The Lord is near. Do not be anxious about anything, but in everything in prayer and petition, with thanksgiving, present your requests to God, and the peace of God, which transcends all understanding, will guard your hearts and your minds in Christ Jesus"*. Just like God gave the Israelites manna everyday (only enough for each day) – God gave mom and me the strength we needed each day.

God revealed to me and Mom His plan – all of the puzzle pieces of the two years leading to my father's passing fell into a clear picture. We realized how powerful Christ in our hearts can be – Ephesians 3:17-19 says, *"Christ may dwell in your hearts through faith. And I pray that you, being rooted and established in love, may have power, together with all the saints, to grasp how wide and long and high and deep is the love of Christ, and to know this love that surpasses knowledge – that you may be filled to the measure of all the fullness of God".* I have such a peace knowing that my dad, as a believer in Jesus Christ, is in Heaven and will have eternal life. John 3:16 says, *"For God so loved the world that he gave his one and only Son, that whoever believes in him shall not perish, but have eternal life."*

In addition to this power of the Holy Spirit - the Lord has given me a boldness to witness like I never thought I would ever have! My 2001 Christmas letter (which barely got mailed due to the darkness outside) was my mild attempt to witness to my friends and family before this tragedy took place. That Christmas letter became a vehicle to share even more with a renewed boldness and it has spread like wildfire. God can even use a piece of paper. Most people received my letter the day before my dad passed away. It has been circulated by fax, email, read over the phone, passed out at parties, given to a pastor in Dallas and he incorporated it into his Christmas message, it was copied and sent in other people's Christmas cards, and both Mom and I copied it for hundreds of people (our entire Bible study classes). I thank God for this boldness and I pray it never ceases. Psalm 138:3 says, *"When I called, you answered me; you made me bold and stouthearted."* I continue to write my annual Christmas letter...Even though I never feel I have anything to say, people continue to tell me it blesses them!

God has also revealed to me in a whole new light as to what is important here on earth. Matthew 6:19-21 says, *"Do not store up for yourselves treasures on earth, where moth and rust destroy, and where thieves break in and steal. But store up for yourselves treasures in heaven where moth and rust do not destroy. For where your treasure is, there your heart will also be."* My heart was too focused on earthly things, but I am so thankful for grace and that because of Jesus I can wash away those sins and focus my heart here on earth with a heavenly focus. Ecclesiastes 5:15 says *"Naked a man comes from his mother's womb and as he comes he so departs. He takes nothing from his labor that he can carry in his hands."*

I have learned that I can help others who are suffering when I myself am suffering. Now I can relate with people who are suffering. I never truly understood before this experience. I remind myself daily to thank God in all circumstances and pray continually. 1 Thessalonians 5:16-18 says, *"Be joyful always; pray continually; give thanks in all circumstances, for this is God's will for you in Christ Jesus."* It is evident to me that there is always someone who has a worse situation than me, and I remind myself daily to keep everything in my life in perspective.

I may have learned all of these things without suffering the sudden loss of my father at a fairly young age, but knowing this early in my life gives me more time to live a life knowing these lessons and more time to serve the Lord in a special, more compassionate way.

On December 5, 2001, my Dad went to sleep as usual with his to-do list on his desk for the next day and instead woke up to the Lord our God in Heaven. I ask you - What is on your to-do list?

Question to you:

Have you accepted the Lord into your heart and do you have the boldness to make sure your loved ones are saved too? Is your item on your to-do list to share the Lord with your Mom? Is there unforgiveness in your heart? Is an item on your to-do list to forgive your Dad or a friend? Don't wait for tomorrow because you don't know if you will awake to your to-do list for tomorrow. Mend your fences now and share the Lord with all you love. I want everyone to feel the peace I feel that comes from the assurance that God is welcoming your loved one into the Kingdom.

If you don't know Christ personally...Is a relationship with our Lord on your to-do list? Are you saying to yourself, I will just go to Sunday school each Sunday until I feel ready to dig deeper? Are you saying maybe next week? Maybe next month? Psalm 90:12 says *"Teach us how short our lives really are so that we may be wise."* Do you realize how short YOUR life really is?

Don't go to sleep thinking you will deal with this tomorrow... as tomorrow may never come!

Are you ready to go to sleep tonight?

Kristina Keller Gray

Christmas Letter from 2001

Dear Friends and Family,

As commercialized as Christmas has become, I continue to remind myself that this season is not about gifts and stocking stuffers or even meals with the family. Christmas is the celebration of the birth of Jesus Christ.

In reflecting on the birth of Jesus, I cannot help but focus on how Jesus is a "gift" to me. I am so undeserving of this gift! The sacrifice God made to send his only son to die so that I may have eternal life is the greatest gift of all. The birth of Christ is the beginning of God's gift to us. When He sent His son to die for us, He tied the bow of the beautifully wrapped package and laid it at our feet. He lets us decide if we want to open the gift and enjoy the blessings tucked inside.

God laid that package at my feet and I received Christ into my heart as a teenager, but I simply undid the bow. It wasn't until about four years ago that I truly accepted the gift of the Lord, tore the wrapping off and with great anticipation opened the box! For me, opening the gift was a complete change in my heart, actions and life. I only realized the content of the package after I was ready to open it...eternal life and the power of the Holy Spirit.

The Holy Spirit gives me the 'fruit' of love, joy, peace, patience, kindness, goodness, gentleness, faithfulness and self-control. What a wonderful gift! I wish I could give each of you such a wonderful gift to celebrate Christmas. Since I cannot do that, the next best thing is to share with you the concept of this wonderful gift and tell you that it is wrapped and waiting for you too.

Have you even realized that you have received the gift? Have you begun to open it and untied only the bow? Or have you torn the pretty wrapping and taken off the lid to reveal the contents inside?

Having this precious gift doesn't mean a life without trials or pain. It does help to equip us to deal with those circumstances. And having this gift with me each and every day gives me strength!

I pray this holiday season is not about Christmas trees, ornaments, expensive presents or even home-cooked meals. I pray this is a time of reflection...A time of forgiveness...A time of repentance...A time of love and kindness...A time of acceptance...A time of remembrance!

Look under your tree this year at the many gifts and honestly ask yourself if you have accepted the only gift that truly matters. For those of you who have, I urge you to dig deeper into the box, searching for and discovering more and more each and everyday.

More importantly, be sure to tell someone else how the gift has changed your life and how it can change theirs too!

May God bless you and your family.
Kristina

> Ephesians 2: 8 *"For it is by grace you have been saved, through faith— and this not from yourselves, it is the gift of God!"*

Safe in Christ

On Friday (Good Friday) I was awakened around 4:30AM by sirens which just kept going and going. I soon realized that it was a warning siren. I woke my husband and we turned on the TV. Sure enough, there were tornado warnings all around us and we were hearing terrific winds, rain and hail. We wondered whether we should take shelter in a safe part of our house. It soon passed over and we went back to bed. We later heard that a tornado had touched down just South of us and then went on to touch down about 30 miles Northeast of us in Murfreesboro, TN killing one young mother and her baby and destroying hundreds of homes.

The entire day was spent watching the TV for more news of storms coming through. Several more tornados touched down, one in the same town (Murfreesboro) as before. There were more homes destroyed and many people injured. It was a terrible day watching the clouds and rain sweep through time after time, all day long.

Saturday dawned cold, dark & rainy. It was just a really gloomy day until around 6:00 PM when it began to clear and we could see some signs of blue skies.

Now it's Sunday! The sun is bright; the temperature is around 68 degrees on the way into the 70's. A beautiful Easter Sunday that we can celebrate our Lord's resurrection.

Why do I tell you this in my Easter message? It reminds me of what was happening to Jesus so many years ago. The tornadoes reminded me of the pain and suffering that happened in His life on the night He was arrested by the Roman soldiers. He was tortured and humiliated all night. His life was in turmoil. Then on Good Friday He hung on the cross all day and suffered, taking on our sin and shame in addition to the physical suffering He was enduring. People watched and waited for the end to come, just as we watched and waited for the end of the stormy day on Friday.

While He lay in the tomb on Saturday, it must have been a cloudy, cold time for everyone just as it was for us on Saturday.

But then on Sunday, the Son rose from the grave and a new light was shining for all to see. He was ALIVE! The light and warmth had returned to the world. A light that could never be extinguished. A light that still shines bright today.

What wonderful hope we now have because the Son is shining for each and every one of us who believe that Jesus died, was buried and rose on the third day.

Enjoy your Easter celebrating the risen Christ. Thank Him for His protection from the storms of life and share His Light with others who may not know Him.

I pray for each of you a Blessed Easter Sunday.

Safe in Christ,

Naomi Ford-Bolt

I Almost Missed It

My story is of a little girl growing up in middle-class America, going to college, getting married, having kids, pursing a career, and going to church. I had loving, caring parents, who instilled in me character traits of hard work, perseverance, and honesty. I married Prince Charming, who swept me off my feet, and we had two of the most adorable, smart, sweet boys you could ever ask for. I have truly been blessed with a wonderful family, friends, career, material possessions, and good health. What more could a person ask for?

Then my husband, Derwood, came home from a spiritual retreat weekend called The Walk to Emmaus, and said I had to go on the Walk! He had already filled out the application and said, "Sign here." He was beside himself; he was so enthusiastic and happy. Derwood said it was one of the top three things in his life, right up there with getting married and having kids.

So, on Mother's Day weekend of 2000, I went on the Walk to Emmaus. I didn't go to find the Lord, but He certainly found me. I have never felt so much love in my whole life. Love, joy, peace and gratitude were overflowing. I'm pretty much a crybaby by nature, but now memories of the Walk, a song, or communion will bring tears streaming down my face. Derwood was right, it was not only top three; it was life-changing!

All those years in church and I had missed it. I thought believing in God made me a Christian. I didn't understand what people meant when they talked about a personal relationship with Jesus. Then it finally became crystal clear: Jesus died on the cross for me! He has just been waiting for me to decide whether I would accept it. How truly humbling to be given a gift of this magnitude. I accepted Jesus with open arms, never wanting to be apart from Him again.

Whole new doors opened up. I went from believing with my head to loving Jesus with my whole heart. Going to church changed from "I should" to "I can't wait". Reading the Bible changed from a parable to the revelation of our living Lord. Work was no longer my all in all.

I soon discovered I was no longer living in a fairy tale world. My carriage had turned into a pumpkin and my ball gown into rags. I realized what a retched sinner I am, and how far I had to go to be like Jesus. So many difficult lessons to learn, sometimes multiple times, such as, "It is not all about me!"

It has been a slow process dying to self, but in other respects very liberating. Just like salvation, I learned I couldn't do it on my own, but had to rely on Jesus. He not only saved my life, but now He is transforming it. Everyday is a new gift in which I am given the opportunity to be a little less self-centered and a little more giving.

Looking back I can see how God had been working in my life all along, how He placed different people and opportunities in my life, especially my Christian roommates in college who I adored, and who finally got me to go to church. I am so thankful we have a faithful Lord who never gives up. While I actively pursued the "good life," I almost missed the best life. But He lovingly governed my direction and navigated my path to find Jesus. At age 44, I accepted Christ as my savior and I was baptized the following year.

Jesus is my Redeemer, my Shepherd, my Hope, my Rock, my Prince of Peace, and my Lord and Savior. **He is now, and forever shall be, my All in All**!

Before I was a believer, I thought I was good enough to go to heaven. Now that really does sound like a fairy tale. My "good enough" is like filthy rags when compared to the holiness and righteousness of God. Only Jesus' death on the cross was enough. No one's good deeds, not even Mother Teresa's, can replace the supreme sacrifice of Jesus.

There are no riches on earth compared to salvation in Jesus. I hope you will open your heart and invite Him in. It is simple and it is life-changing. Then go tell someone whom you want to know Jesus.

"*For God so loved the world that He gave His one and only Son, that whoever believes in Him shall not perish but have eternal life.*"
- John 3:16

Gail Anderson

In Jesus Love,

Sold Out

M y greatest achievement as a parent is that all of my children are Christians. Those of you who are struggling with rebellious children can take to heart the scripture from Proverbs 22:6 which says, *"Train up a child in the way he should go and when he is old, he will not depart from it."* Also, take strength from the scripture in Galatians 6:9, *"And let us not be weary in well doing: for in due season we shall reap, if we faint not."* I know only too well how hard it is to raise Christian children in our world today, but the word of God does promise us success.

Now let's back up about 44 years to Grand Prairie, Texas, where, when I was about 12 years old I heard Jesus knock on the door of my heart during a service at the Methodist church, and I gladly gave him my heart. I don't remember anything of that service except hearing the voice of Jesus saying, come unto me. Shortly thereafter I was baptized and I wish I could say that from that point I always followed Jesus with all of my heart but I can't. I was like the sower *"who heard the word and with joy received it, yet he had no root in himself, and endureth for a while, but when tribulation or persecution arose because of the word, he drifted away."* (Matthew 13:21) I think that in my Methodist church we didn't have a lot of teaching on what to do after we gave our lives to Jesus. Or at least I wasn't listening to it. What followed for me were teenage years of following Jesus from afar. My family was regular church goers but we didn't really talk about our relationships with God, pray, or read the Bible together. Therefore, I never thought to have a more personal relationship with Jesus. I didn't know he could do anything practical in this life except save me from hell (though at this stage in life I think that's pretty practical.)

Then, during my senior year of high school I met Charley. He was the first person in my circle of friends who really knew about practical things that God could do for you. Now mothers, take heart here, Charley was raised up as a young man in the way he should go. Granted, he wasn't really following God anymore than I was, but he did have some knowledge of the working of the Holy Spirit in people's lives because his parents were very spiritual people. When I met them and they talked to me about Jesus, I knew they had something much more than I did, and they won me over with their genuine love for me. To me they lived the exhortation in the scripture to love the unlovely because I know I wasn't the girl of their dreams for their son at that time. I had grown up in a very unaffectionate home where I had to earn my parents' approval (my parents loved me dearly but had been raised this way themselves) and here Charley's parents were people who just loved me where I was, and this really impressed me. Well, as God would have it, in spite of our lack of commitment to God at this time, he still had mercy on us, and Charley and I were married in November of 1968. Shortly after this, his parents moved to Guadalajara, Mexico to become missionaries. Though they had gone, the good seed had been sown in my heart through them. Matthew 13:23, *"But he that received seed into the good ground is he that hears the word of God and understands it and goes on to bear fruit with his life"*. This move left Charley and me with little spiritual guidance and lots of newlywed problems. Where was I going to find answers to these problems? Since this was the late sixties (the decade of peace and love), it was a time of searching for us and all of our peers in college. I began to seek a daily relationship with the same Jesus that had saved me so many years before. We had a saying in the sixties about being "sold out" to something and the best thing I ever did for myself was to totally sell out to Jesus Christ. In those days of the Jesus movement fervor everything was all or nothing and I made a real commitment to Jesus. We had a practice at this time to pray something through and I simply gave my whole heart and soul to Jesus and promised to follow him all the rest of my life as long as he would show me the things he wanted me to do in a way that I could understand. Did it work? Yes, it did. Will it work for you? Yes, it will. How do I know? Because the Bible says in Hebrews 13:8, *"Jesus Christ, the same yesterday, and today, and forever."* I wish I could tell you all the ways that Jesus has been involved in my life on a day-to-day basis since that time, but my focus is not just my life, but yours. I have heard many wonderful testimonies of women who are so attractive, smart, and spiritual. I know it looks as though they are so together, but I know they are willing to say along with me that we didn't start out that way. Probably between us all our sins would line up from here to heaven. Let me say that I know that God is no respecter of persons, and what he has done for me he will do for you. Whether you know it or not, you have already started a journey toward Jesus by beginning to learn about Jesus through the word of God. But knowing the word of God is not enough, you must have a personal relationship with Jesus. If you are not sure that you have given your life to Jesus, to save you and fill you with His Holy Spirit, let me encourage you to do this today. All God is looking for is your willingness to ask him to come into your heart, to be sorry for the things you have done that are wrong, and to look to him for direction. After you have done this, please share your decision with someone who is a believer who you can trust. The scripture encourages us to do this in Revelation12:11 when it says, *"And they overcame by the blood of the Lamb (the blood Jesus shed on the cross for our sin) and by the word of their testimony."* Why don't you sell out to Jesus today? It is the single most important decision you will ever make.

Gwen McMath

Perfect Timing

My wife of 43 years, Nancy Alexander, was taken to the hospital by ambulance on January 2, 2009. She died of acute pneumonia, complicated by post-polio syndrome, on January 10, 2009.

God helped us and comforted us through this very difficult time in our lives. I don't know how we could have made it through this with out God's help, comfort, and guidance.

The five days she was in ICU are a blur. I kept in touch with family and friends to let them know that Nancy was in ICU in critical condition and I visited her during the allowed specified times.

In quiet times at home during this time the chorus to a song kept running through my mind. I knew that God was there and he was comforting me through the words to the song, "As the Deer" by Martin Nystrom. Taken from the Psalms, it refers to the Lord as "my strength and shield," and speaks of yielding one's spirit.

Nancy was on a ventilator in ICU and the doctors only gave her a 50/50 chance of breathing on her own once the breathing tube was pulled out.

On the day the ventilator was to be removed there were family, friends, and three ministers gathered in Nancy's small ICU room, approximately twenty people in all.

Before the procedure to remove her breathing tube we sang hymns, read scripture, had communion, our minister anointed Nancy with oil, and we prayed. Nancy had not been awake or responsive the entire time she was in ICU. One of our friends standing at the foot of Nancy's bed asked her if she wanted the 23rd Psalm read? To everyone's surprise Nancy nodded her head yes.

This was the only time, to anyone's knowledge, that she was awake or responsive during her time in the hospital and in hospice. I know this was a <u>God moment</u> because the 23rd Psalm was very important to Nancy. Nancy quoted the 23rd Psalm to her mother when she died in 1991 and she read the same Psalm to her grandmother when she died in 2008 at the age of 106.

After they removed the breathing tube Nancy was able to breath on her own, but it was shallow and labored.

One day when my daughter came into the hospice room she said she heard a song on her way there that meant a lot to her. She knew that God was there and he was comforting her through the words to that song.

The title of the song was "There Will Be a Day", and part of the chorus says that there will be a day, when we will have no more pain, tears, or fears, and we will see Jesus again.

My daughter asked if we could get that same local radio station on the computer. My son-in-law tuned in another Christian radio station from out of town that he preferred. The first song they played after their commercial was "There Will Be a Day". We all knew that God was there and he was comforting us through the words to that song.

Nancy's breathing was very shallow and she would not take a breath for short periods of time.

On the afternoon of January 10, 2009 there were myself, our three kids, and their spouses sitting around Nancy's bed. Our son and one of our sons-in-law had stayed with Nancy the last two nights and they were telling us about a funny event that had happened the night before. We were all laughing and cutting up when we looked over at Nancy and she was not breathing. We waited to see if she would take another breath but she was gone. It was approximately 4:00 pm.

God put the thoughts in my mind of stories I had read of people having out-of-body experiences. When they died they floated up to the ceiling and could see everything going on in the room.

When Nancy died I hope she could see her family beside her, laughing and cutting up, because that is <u>*exactly*</u> how she would have wanted to go. She was always so full of life; she could see that her family was there, and be comforted with the knowledge that we could carry on as a family without her. God was so gracious to allow us the time to grieve, to express how much we loved her and to tell her goodbye.

God's timing is _perfect_. If it had been up to us we would have let her go when the breathing tube was pulled out. But that would not have allowed us the special time we had with her or the special way she left us as we were laughing and cutting up as a family.

God's timing is always perfect.

Rudy Alexander

Jesus Saves One of His Family Members

Born in Upstate New York into a Conservative Jewish family, I was the oldest of three boys. I always believed in God, but thought that Jesus Christ was at best the Christian God and at worst, something I said when I was angry! I believed that the New Testament was an Anti-Semitic book, Mary was a Catholic, and John was a Baptist. There was nothing else I had to know about the matter. Jews and Jesus didn't mix!

There were quite a few Jews living in my town, and I don't remember ever hearing an Anti-Semitic comment. But when I was 13, that all changed. After my Bar Mitzvah, we moved to another town in Upstate New York, and I found myself in 7th grade as the only Jew in the school. It was then that I heard my first Anti-Semitic comment. One boy said to another, "You dirty Jew!" I was shocked! I asked him what he said and he told me he was not talking to me but to another boy! He had no idea what he was saying but knew he was saying it as a curse upon the other boy! Having already thought that all non-Jews were Christian, I thought all Christians hated Jews! Only a few years later I found out it wasn't true.

At 17 I had a girlfriend who said she was Christian, but she and her family were different. They seemed to love and accept me because I was Jewish! That was new! I started thinking that maybe not all Christians were Jew-haters!

I graduated high school and went to college in another city in Upstate New York. At that time I got to be a pretty good sinner. I could down beers with the best of them, and I also couldn't say a sentence without a dirty word! Not the kind of guy that God could be proud of! I still thought I was a good guy doing what I should be doing, but in reality I was going farther from being a "good guy" in God's eyes!

In my sophomore year, the Lord brought another Christian to be my roommate. He was a simple guy who also seemed to appreciate me for being Jewish. Jim and I had some pretty good talks, but nothing he said really made me think that I could accept this Jesus that he believed in.

After graduating college, I looked for a job in my field of meteorology, and found one in Pennsylvania. I was one of the low men on the totem pole, making almost minimum wage. It was there the Lord sent other real Christians into my path, and I could see how different they really were! They even told me they were praying for me! I guess they saw I really needed the Lord!

I enjoyed working in my field, but not for minimum wage! After about a year working there, I decided it was time to leave. I said goodbye to my Christian buddies, and moved on. I got a job in another field, and they sent me to Mexico to work as a surveying assistant. Because I had become a great sinner by that time, I lost my job after just a few weeks! I went back to the US, and then back to Mexico a few months later. After losing my job a second time, I found myself in Mexico "peso-less" but wanting to stay there. I finally found a job as an English teacher at a language institute in Guadalajara.

I really enjoyed being a teacher, as I got a lot of respect, but my sinning got even worse. Even though I was going to the Synagogue a few times a month, I was still sinking into worse despair. God continued to send committed Christians into my path, and I continued to see that maybe there was something to this Christianity. They behaved like nice people, not like me!

My situation got even worse after I started to hear voices. When I would say a bad word or do another sin, I heard a voice saying, "I don't like that, don't do it!" But then I heard another voice saying, "Yeah, do it, everyone's doing it!" Finally the voice saying I shouldn't do it got stronger, and I realized I was doing something wrong. But I didn't have any power within myself to stop doing those sinful acts. I was in such turmoil I couldn't even live with myself anymore! I needed a change!

I started going to the Synagogue a bit more, and it did help a little. Hearing the Old Testament read was a small help, but I still had the sin nature within me. I got so desperate I thought I would try almost anything. I finally thought that maybe there was something to this Christianity. I actually got enough guts to walk into one of my Christian co-worker's office and asked him about "his religion." He was shocked, seeing the Lord answer his prayers for me, but proceeded to tell me that God really loves the Jews. He gave me a few scriptures to read in the Old Testament, which I did gladly. It was there that I saw that God really loves the Jews. I had read it before in the Synagogue, but I finally understood it for myself!

I went back to Mike and thanked him. Then he told me to read from the New Testament. I told him absolutely not! He told me that if I didn't read it, I would never find the solution to my dilemma. More inner conflict! Finally after a few weeks of fighting about "turning my back on Judaism", I decided I had to do the unthinkable. I opened the New Testament! To my amazement, Jesus was Jewish and the New Testament wasn't an Anti-Semitic book! They lied to me! After reading the New Testament I realized that Jesus was great for the Christians, but still wasn't convinced that as a Jew I could accept Him into my life.

But then, I saw just how much Jesus loved His people, the Jews, and how I was a sinner and only through Jesus could I get free! Then came the real clincher! I read John 14:6, where Jesus says that He's the way, the truth and the life, and nobody gets to the Father except by Him. I said, "Not even me, God?"

His reply was a shocker, "Especially not you!" I knew that I was in trouble then. I asked the Lord, "What about my family?" He said that He would take care of them. I then said I wanted to see one more Jewish person who had accepted Him, and I would also!

When I told my Christian friends, they said that they just happened to know a Messianic Jewish woman living in the city, and they would set up a meeting with a few of us. I said ok, and about 7 of us went to a restaurant. When she walked into the restaurant, I saw joy and peace on her face that I didn't have. I asked her a few questions and then we all went our separate ways. That evening, I told God I had no more excuses, confessed my sins and I gave my life to Yeshua! (Jesus!) The change was almost immediate! He took away my desire for alcohol and the swear words were erased from my vocabulary! Yeshua saved this Jew!

That was more than 27 years ago and I am still walking with Yeshua, now serving Him in Israel! Don't you want to see your family members saved? So does Jesus! Pray for the Jewish people to accept our Messiah and accept His forgiveness just as I have! God bless you!

Avi Schwartz, Israel

Holes in the Darkness

As the oldest of four children growing up in an alcoholic family, I didn't understand that I have nothing to prove because God is so big He can cover the whole world with His grace and love and yet so small, He can curl up inside my heart. I felt it was my responsibility to be in control and restore order to the chaos, to star in the fantasy of pretending that my family was normal; and to stand up to the emotional abuse by protecting the weak. I decided at a very early age that one day, somehow, I would defy the odds and break free from those chains by doing everything the right way, following all the rules, and live happily ever after....

I will always be grateful to my parents for dropping us kids off almost every Sunday morning at the front door of the largest Baptist church in town. As you can well imagine, being from the other side of the tracks, we stuck out like a sore thumb! During the sixth grade, I accepted Jesus as my Savior during a very dramatic evangelism service complete with real fire shooting out of some sort of contraption used to demonstrate what would happen should I ever decide to journey off of a very straight and narrow path. I wasn't taking any chances and was the first one down the isle! Please don't get me wrong, the foundation was laid and my love for Jesus (as well as a healthy dose of fear!) was the only thing I could truly count on during a very difficult time.

During the early years of my marriage, my husband and I attended various churches off and on but when I had my first child, it suddenly became imperative that we find a church home. Remember, I was doing everything I could to break the cycle of my childhood. Again the busyness of life pulled us in different directions, and there was always that softball tournament or camping trip that called our names on weekends. In addition, we were battling the system trying to find resources for a son with ADHD and learning disabilities during a time when very little was known about that diagnosis. Once again my family just didn't quite seem to fit in with "normal" church folks and there I was, it seemed, on the outside looking in. As I look back, I can see now that it was my own brokenness and lack of self-worth that made me feel so isolated.

Nine years later, my daughter was born, and we were back in church, thanks to the "casserole lady" who had never given up on us! It was also during this time that I attended the Walk to Emmaus, a Christian retreat, which I truly believe was one of the most freeing, life-changing spiritual events in my life. Finally, all the pieces of the puzzle fit, the cloud of confusion and doubt was lifted, and I didn't have to carry that heavy burden of saving the world any more! I felt a renewed commitment to trust God's calling from complacency to involvement. Instead of pleading my inadequacies, I accepted God's urgings to use my organizational skills by serving as a leader on several committees and projects. I have to confess that my transformation did not happen overnight as I still battled unrealistic personal expectations and my need for perfection. Through prayer and the love and wisdom of treasured friends, I realized that this was more about me and not about God and that I had allowed those deep feelings of inadequacy from the past to permeate my very being.

I have always been touched by the Biblical concepts of light and darkness, and several years ago I heard a message on Christian radio that has forever left an imprint on my heart. Ron Hutchcraft shared the story of a very young Robert Louis Stevenson who was observed looking intently out the window one night, oblivious to the world around him. He was watching a lamplighter making his way down the street, lighting one street lamp after another, and excitedly exclaimed, "Look at that man! He's punching holes in the darkness!"

Wow, did the light bulb turn on for me at that very moment! What an awesome visual image... God did not put us here to shake our heads and complain how dark it is in our marriages, where we work, or go to church. We are here to punch holes in the darkness, not only for ourselves, but also for those who so desperately need the brilliant light of Jesus Christ to be able to get out of the darkness themselves! How will we choose to share this Light? Will we be contagious in our joy or cranky in our faith? Grateful or grumpy? Will we see the rainbow or the rainstorm? In Matthew 5:14-16, Jesus says, *"You are the light of the world... a city on a hill cannot be hidden. Neither do people light a lamp and put it under a bowl. Instead they put it on its stand, and it gives light to everyone in the house. In the same way, let your light shine before men, that they may see your good deeds and praise your Father in heaven."* Yes, it is a tall order, but we may very well be someone else's best chance of heaven!

I have always tried to keep that visual image of the lamplighter in my heart, and I must admit that sometimes I am more successful than others. We all have experienced our own version of the "dark night of the soul"; when the light of Christ seems to barely flicker, when the world challenges our faith. During these times, we must hold on to the conviction that God knows more than we do about this life and that He will get us through it! And isn't that a warm, comforting feeling!

Linda Hicks

Who am I?

I'm nobody special, just an ordinary girl going through life as a child of the King. God's love and grace is what has got me to this point in my life.

I grew up in a loving Christian home with church every Sunday. I was saved and asked Christ in my heart at a young age and baptized at 12. So where did I get so off course?

As a teenager I thought I was always right and everyone was wrong. My teenage years stopped at 16. I will never forget the disappointment and shock on my mother's face after the doctor said I was pregnant. At 16, my sophomore year, I had to make adult decisions. Abortion…nope, never an option to me. The baby's father was not in the picture. The only option was adoption. The process was very hard, but I found a Christian agency that did open adoptions. On June 1990 I gave birth to a beautiful baby girl. What a bittersweet moment in my life. I just wanted to hold her and never let go, but I knew that it was not God's will. Throughout the years I have received letters and pictures that I still cherish today. One of my favorite moments was witnessing my beautiful daughter graduate and introduce me as, "my mom, Becky." What a joy!

While I was pregnant I started dating a boy from school who was not the baby's father. On July 1990, he asked me to marry him and went off to Army Basic Training. I did not realize then, but I was drifting away from my parents, who were my spiritual support.

We married over Spring Break in 1991. Warren was born in December 1991. Marriage and motherhood at a young age was hard. A lot of tears and phone calls followed to my mom for advice. Two years later Ashley was born and my husband deployed to Korea for a year. During this deployment we lived with my parents and I was back to my Christian roots. After Korea came Germany.

Jenna was born in September 1995. Germany was hard with many deployments and being so far away from my support until I found a church to attend. That helped keep me strong and sane. Finally, reassignment to Fort Hood, Texas, we attended church at first and then it became easier not to go.

Our marriage began to deteriorate, and we began to make destructive choices. I spent a lot of my free time with friends at clubs and very little time at church. I asked for a divorce, losing some friends in the process. In God's eyes what I was doing was wrong and it wasn't easy. This was also hard on our four great kids.

After another dysfunctional marriage, I was depressed and disappointed with my choices and wondered how I could ever recover. My mom reminded me, "God will not give you more than you can handle." My response was, "I think God forgot what I am capable of handling!"

Everyone's life is different and we all take different paths. Why I took the paths I did does not matter anymore. What does matter is learning from those mistakes. My parents always pointed out God's blessings in my life, but I had pushed God aside. I always knew He was there but I did not look to Him like I should have. I found a great church in January 2006. Slowly I started getting plugged in and made friends. Eventually I started seeing changes in my life. Forgiving others who have hurt me and my children has taken a while, but with God's help I'm doing it. The best thing I have done is to start serving in church. My faith is stronger and my friends have grown in numbers. Most of all, God has blessed me more abundantly than I ever dreamed. I have met a wonderful man, Tom, who also serves in our church. He helps me to seek God first and encourages me to be a stronger Christian. God has great plans for me as long as I keep Him Lord of my life.

Rebecca Ryschon

Glory to God Alone

I can remember the thrill of attending my first Yankee game at the age of nine in 1947. Taking the bus from College Point to Flushing; walking down several flights of stairs to the Main Street Station where my parents and I boarded the subway. Within a minute the train emerged from underground onto the elevated tracks and traveled east until it reached the East River. The train went underground again and we disembarked at Grand Central Station where we went up several steep escalators to the Lexington Line and boarded the Woodlawn-Jerome subway. We made our way to the first car where I stood enthralled as the dimly lit tracks and pillars rushed toward me until finally the train emerged from the darkness onto the elevated tracks, the majestic Yankee Stadium suddenly appearing bigger than life beside the station at 161st. Street.

Once in the ballpark, I saw for the first time, in their traditional pinstripe livery, the greatest team in baseball, THE NEW YORK YANKEES. I looked up to and emulated these athletes when I was a boy, and nothing I have discovered has or ever will change my attitude toward them. It is one thing that has enriched my life and allowed me to transcend the realities of everyday life. Over the next 18 years, the Yankees rewarded my allegiance with 15 American League pennants, losing only in 1948 and (despite winning 103 games) in 1954 to the Cleveland Indians, and then in 1959 to the Chicago White Sox. During those 15 Fall Classic appearances from 1947 through 1964, the Yankees won 10 World Series Championships. It was difficult for me **not** to assume that God was a Yankee fan.

The Yankees have dominated the game of baseball from the glory of "Babe" Ruth and the "Iron Man" Lou Gehrig, to the grace of Joe DiMaggio, to the reign of Mickey Mantle and Casey Stengel, through the turmoil of Reggie Jackson, Thurman Munson and Billy Martin, to the 1998 World Champion team with their 125 total victories and into the twenty-first century teams of Jeter and A-Rod.

In 1998, I realized my dream of playing "with" (notice I did not say "for") the New York Yankees when I attended their Fantasy Camp. At the particular camp I attended, the 1961 infield was featured.

One of my earliest recollections of that week was when I put on the Yankee uniform for the first time and walked by a mirror in the locker room. While I am not implying any sacredness to the Yankee livery, I realized that the momentary joy I experienced was but a mere finite shadow of the infinite joy I will have when one day I stand clothed in the righteous of Christ.

It was a thrill to play and meet with one of my all-time Yankee favorites Bobby Richardson. Between games each day we would eat in the locker room where I was honored when another of all-time Yankee favorite of mine, shortstop and later NBC announcer Tony Kubek, would sit with me to discuss theological issues.

Each night we would all gather around and toss questions at these Yankee legends. One evening someone asked Don Mattingly if he thought he had "retired one year too early?" Mattingly was one of the greatest first basemen in Yankee history having played for them from late 1982 through his retirement year of 1995; years in which the Yankees did not play in the World Series. The year following Mattingly's retirement the Yankees won it all, thus the reason for the question being asked of him.

Mattingly, who at that time had hair down to his shoulders and sported a Fu-Manchu moustache, did not answer immediately. Then he gave an answer that I'll never forget. Mattingly said, "No," paused, and then added, "I never look back and ask why, but rather I always look up and give thanks." All of the world's greatest sermons have never said so much in so few words. Soli Deo Gloria!

Paul A. Tambrino, Ed.D., Ph.D.

The Spirit of the
Most High God

I grew up knowing about God. My parents taught me from their own understanding, according to how they were raised and what God had been trying to show them. But of course, there comes a time in everyone's life when we become accountable for ourselves to the One and Only True and Most High Living God of Heaven and of Earth. That time, for me, arrived in December of 2001 when my husband and I separated and later divorced.

It was at that time that I had to reflect on who I was, where I had come from, and what in the world had just happened. My husband and I had both grown up with spiritual leadership and we had performed the religious rituals asked of us, like attending church, tithing, giving of ourselves, and living seemingly normal Christian lives. But what I failed to mention was that for me, this was all an act, a religious act, a self-deceived view of a "good Christian" girl who only knew *about* God and never really *knew* Him.

I had so many faults, but never realized them until my husband was gone. I honestly could say that I truly felt I was a precious gift to the man and that he had just never realized it. It's funny now, but was a very painful realization back then. I began to question God a lot! I prayed to Him constantly and only a few months later, He blessed me with an out-of-body experience that I can hardly describe with my limited wisdom, knowledge, and understanding of the heavenly realm! Jesus greeted me there, in a garden I can only presume to be His original Garden of Eden. He was not man, but a welcoming Being in a spiritual, glorified body of pure light. He said He was so glad I had finally come to visit, and I was more than delighted and full of His great joy, His vast love, and His unconceivable peace (none of which I had ever experienced in my life, until that very moment). As He got up, "Daddy" gracefully towered over my miniature light-being self and reached for my hand...which I realized had become one great light, my internal spirit connection with Him! He showed me many things that I had misunderstood about Him and about our earthly life, and He devalued the many gods I once served, like money, TV, businesses, jobs, houses, things, even people. He opened my eyes to spirit, soul, and body, and took away the evil, deceptive spirit that had been living in me for years.

After this experience, I actually got worse instead of better, but only to the natural eye, because He was doing a work inside of me. He was healing, forgiving, and correcting me spiritually, and because of the overwhelming task that lay ahead for me, in all the other areas of my life: mentally, emotionally, physically, etc. He blessed me with an analogy. He said picture yourself as a turtle, with the shell representing your body, your spirit being represented by the actual reptile inside of the shell, and your mind and emotions being the substance that glues that tortoise to the shell. While the reptile now has a new glorified body on the inside the exterior shell visible to the outside world is still filthy. He told me He would take the scaled portions on that shell, one by one, and thoroughly clean them out. As one is repaired, cleaned, polished and waxed, it is put back and another is ready to go through the same process. Eventually, I will make my way around the entire exterior of the shell, pulling and correcting the substance (thinking) that is connected to the new glorified self on the inside, as well. He said to not worry about the process or get upset that people will still notice those areas He has not transformed yet. Concentrate and focus on Him, and others will begin to notice those new sparkling, shiny areas of wisdom, knowledge, understanding, compassion, tolerance, peace, joy, love, and forgiveness that have been conquered and cleansed, and you will be a blessing and a witness. What a good and merciful and loving God we serve!

So, life continued and I began volunteering in church more and going to Bible College and reading and praying and practically living at church every day. Eventually, I got burned out. I was focusing again on the things I was supposed to be doing or felt I should be doing, instead of focusing on what God had originally told me in my experience with

Him. You see, He called me to do something. I had forgotten how I had begged for Him to keep me there with Him and argued that I was nobody of significant value for Him to send me back to this world. I had nothing to my name but debt, no degrees or business successes, no accolades, just an overweight mother of two young sons. Oh, that was it…my two young sons. Who was going to teach them about God, The One and Only Worthy God? Who was going to make the corrections in their thinking and rebuke the generational curses that I had allowed to be birthed in them? Who else was going to have that desire? So, He told me, "Go and tell everyone about this experience with Me and tell them that I love them". That is it! That's all He wanted me to do, and I was doing everything except that! I was doing my own thing, my way, and that is why I got burned out. I didn't even want to attend church any more, because I already knew Him, and I wondered if that was why other men and women had stopped attending church. I asked Him one day, "What would bring us, the church, back, and keep us from losing our desire to minister?" And He answered, of course! But He answered by asking me a question, "What feeds you?" Well, that answer was simple for me. What feeds me is hearing other people's "coming to Jesus" moments. Hearing different testimonies of how God has saved them, forgiven them, blessed them, healed them, and delivered them! Remembering His goodness, His love, and His blessings as I tell others of my very own experiences with Him! That is what feeds me! That is what motivates me, that is what brings me to my knees in humility towards this Omnipotent Being, this Omniscient Spirit, this Most High God who has created us and opened up our eyes and given us wisdom beyond understanding. That is what feeds me! That is what breathes life and reminds me of my own walk with Him!

The Bible is filled with many testimonies of men and women throughout the Old and New Testaments, and stories of how God has intervened in their lives for their good. And the greatest testimony of all is that of Jesus Christ and how His blood has redeemed us. What better way to honor God and what He has done in our lives, than by sharing our testimony with others, which is what He exhorts us ALL to do in His Word, and what He revealed to me was my ministry. I was led to set up a weekly event, not to interfere with the regular church services, but to be an additional night of sharing our experiences with one another. Where people from all denominations and backgrounds would come together to hear the goodness of what God has done and to tell about His goodness in their own life. It was a few years after my walk with Him in the "Garden of Eden" and yet another year after this Testimony Night vision that I would venture out to begin Testimony Night. I had seen so many hurting people that I knew would be blessed by this ministry (especially a coworker and very good friend of mine), and that finally moved me to hold this event, even if it meant it would only be the two of us at the local Whataburger. That night, after the event, she gave her life to God, and she has an amazing testimony of her own. We currently hold these meetings monthly and will soon be back to our weekly schedule.

What a deserving and loving God, who asks nothing of us but to share His love with the world. He took an ignorantly deceived religious girl and turned her into a loving child of The Most High God, and He is still working on me and my part in His kingdom work. I thank Him every day and pray that my testimony has brought you to the realization of the ministry He has in, through, and for you....In the Name of Christ Jesus, Our Father in Heaven, through His Holy Spirit, Amen.

Adrina

Testimony to My Lord

As a result of being asked for a testimony of Jesus' love and grace I have been thinking about how he has appeared in my life. Is it about creation and the gleaning of a lesson? How about the moment when suddenly before me God reveals Himself? How about coming through a hardship, self-created or not, with the ability to thank God? I believe all of these events have occurred at some time or another in my life…perhaps many times, and in many ways, and sometimes even recognizable to me.

There was a time that I was not only a sinner but I lived by sin. I was a liar and a thief. I was selfish and I had great pride based on sinful abilities. Most importantly my mind was shut off to any and all righteousness through denial of God and the delusion that the Word was not meant for me. This was manifested in drug and alcohol abuse and addiction which eventually and inevitably led to arrest and incarceration – more than once.

I will never forget the last time I was taken into custody. The procedure at the time was that after booking I was led to a "holding facility" while aspects of my case were considered by the legal system and those assigned to administer that system. The inhabitants of *these* cells are not awarded some of the rights that are given prisoners in the general population where their case disposition has been determined and they are awaiting trial or release or are simply serving their time. At this stage lock down (time in your assigned cell) is 23 out of 24 hours with the remaining hour segmented into meal and hygiene time. There is no television or reading material allowed. I can still feel the dejection as I made my way through booking, uniform issuance, fingerprinting, and the obligatory one telephone call. As the door of my 6' x 10' cell closed I felt singled out as there was no one sharing my cell at that time. I looked at the plastic mats on the two cots, the stainless steel toilet/lavatory unit, and turned to look out the eight by twelve inch window inlaid with steel mesh. I sat on my bunk and was at the lowest point I never hoped to be. I was left alone with my unaltered mind…something I was unaccustomed to and unprepared for. I thought, "God, if you could only give me something to ease my frustration, bewilderment, terror, and despair." As I began to look around the cell I was moved to lift the plastic mats off the steel cots. Where I had been sitting and where I had said this feeble prayer I found a jail issue New Testament. There in a wing in a correctional facility, among 90 or more other arrestees, locked in a cell with no way out, God had revealed Himself to me by delivering His Word. I began to read…

Today I am blessed to know that miracles occur time and time again…both in my life and in the lives of us all. Similarly, I am grateful that my definition of miracles has grown through getting to know my Father, His Spirit, and His Son. It is fairly inclusive from the breath I draw to the things that happen to me that I used to call luck or favorable coincidence. I also thank God that the recognition of miracles as God's grace is awakened within my heart much quicker than it once was. There are many examples of my life how Jesus has been present. My family's intervention was an example of the strength of God in their lives.

My closest brother in age is also one of my best friends. He had brought to my attention his personal concern with my drug and alcohol abuse. I had dismissed his concerns with the usual statements an addict can muster. "I am okay. I'll take it easier. Thank you for caring. I am only hurting myself. It's none of your damn business what I do.", etcetera, etcetera. Without my knowing he confided in my family, perhaps exposing more of his recreational patterns than he might have wanted to. He scheduled a meeting with an intervention counselor and spent hours researching treatment facilities. The intervention was scheduled and all that was left was to get me there without letting me know what was occurring. My wife at the time was in on it and though I was estranged from her she agreed to be the decoy. I was told that I was going to a marriage counseling session. As I pulled into the parking lot of the professional building where this was to take place I noticed my brother. I thought that was strange. I then saw my brother-in-laws pickup truck – very old and unmistakably orange. I realized what was happening and fearing the unknown I bolted. At the end of my wits, I started driving west. For hours I drove the back roads from Lake Buchanan to San Angelo where I spent my last dime on a cheap hotel. I talked a friend into wiring me $200 which I quickly had stolen as I tried to secure illegal drugs. Somewhere deep inside me I must have realized I could not go on and I placed a call home. My brother answered and somehow he talked me into returning. The following week I went to the intervention. More to appease those who loved me I agreed to go to a treatment center although I was not happy. That was the beginning of a long road of recovery. While for a long time I cursed that day and resented my family for putting me through that I now see it as a series of miracles. A blessing! God was working in the lives of those around me so that I may live and serve His purpose. Today I am grateful for many things that I have encountered along the way. Although, as many events have occurred, I have complained and wondered where God was in my life, today I see His hand in each of those instances. As a result when I encounter a hardship today I know that is something God is giving me to learn and grow from. I believe that miracles do not always come in pretty packages.

As I finish this testimony to Jesus I must confess I cannot separate His love and grace from that of God and the Holy Spirit. They are one in my heart and soul. I admit there is much I don't understand about their relationship to each other and perhaps it is best that way. I know that I do my best to walk in His will, and to know His power, and His love. This walk with God sustains me.

Every morning I get up and prepare for a new day. In the course of this I put on shoes and as I do, I am acutely aware of them. I contemplate their color, their amount of wear, their comfort, and their adequacy for the day's activities. I remain cognizant of my shoes for a few steps: Is the right shoe on the left foot? Are they properly strapped or laced? Are there any foreign objects digging into my sole (soul)? The fact that I don't ponder the existence of my shoes minute by minute does not lessen their life value. They are there even when I am not aware of them. Many times throughout the day I am grateful for my shoes. Like, when I have to traipse across a smoldering August parking lot sprinkled with embers of broken glass, or bump into one of those pesky steel rods that seem to worm their way out of old concrete curbs and side-walks. Occasionally, I will be walking across a lush green lawn with nary a twig or leaf in sight, and I'll be tempted to remove my restraining foot covers – until I step on a spot that is none too innocently softer than the rest of the turf. Once again I am glad for my shoes. I believe it is a good idea to always put on your shoes before leaving home.

I wonder too about my awareness of spirituality in life. Gratefully, I no longer question my faith or the power and omnipresence of God. My concern is not that He is always in my life, but that I am aware of Him only at certain times. I know He is with me when I pray upon awakening and before lying down. I recognize Him at various times of the day when I need His help and some of the times that good things happen and, on occasion, when events that I used to call coincidences occur. But is this enough? I fear that a lot of the time I take Him for granted. Perhaps that is the nature of human selfishness.

There have been periods where I have been blessed with an inordinate amount of quiet time - opportunity to be aware of God's presence. As I move further and further from these moments of solitude and commence to follow a process, I hold hope of being deposited on the terraces of normal existence, whatever that may be. As a result, competition for habitation space in my mind adds to confusion. It seems spiritual awareness is crowded out or pushed to the back of the room. Is this the irony of evil? It seems the more I need Him, the less time I have for Him. The answer, then, must be to consciously heighten awareness of God the busier I become. As life becomes hectic I must reach out for His hand more and never be too busy to place the call to Him. As my daily timepiece ticks among dozens of deadlines, I must set aside more moments for Him and not less.

And when things bear down on me, perhaps I shall put on my shoes and go for a walk.

Randy Reed

Angels. Yes, Angels!

Exodus 23:20 *"See, I am sending an angel ahead of you to guard you along the way and to bring you to the place I have prepared."*

We are told that God will protect us to ensure we get to the place He has already prepared. I believe it, I know it, I am excited daily as I see God's hand move on our behalf in ways we could never know. My story is a wonderful story of God's love and grace, and His protection for me and my family based upon many years of praying, failing, yet believing that God's promises are true.

When I was three, I first encountered an angel from the Lord. Yes, at three. This angel spoke to me that he would always be with me. The "voice" I heard and "view" I saw was not normal, but I knew it was something special, powerful, sure, and that it was just for me. At the time, I did not really know all that it meant, but I do remember feeling really safe, loved and protected.

Growing up, my life would encounter many challenges and so many opportunities to be strengthened in my faith or to ignore God's hand and protection. I have seen many things, both good and bad, but I have also experienced the love and protection of God upon my life and the lives of those I know ... family, friends, and communities. I have experienced angels on numerous occasions and, even as I type this note, feel lightheaded from God's overwhelming love for me, His grace and peace. A hand lightly sits on my right shoulder right now.

Because there are so many instances of God's angels in my life, I have decided to use the military style of writing and use bullets to share **some** examples (there have been many more than listed) that will hopefully encourage others:

- Encountered an angel at three years old. Assured me that He would always be with me. Has guarded and protected me from many things throughout my life and I have felt angels so many times and see their works on my behalf. **Results:** He accepted me as His child and I have been His ever since.
- At 13, when I wanted to scream at another person for their (what I believed to be their) wrongs and unfairness to me and my family, an angel touched my cheek ever so lightly and whispered "Be still, I am here with you and everything will be okay." **Results:** He taught me to forgive, unconditionally, and I am so free because of it.

- At 17 when things seemed to be confused and falling apart in my life and it seemed as though there was absolutely nothing I could do to change it, as I cried out in bed for help, God's angel appeared in the room and such comfort came over me that I never again feared what could be, but became excited about what will be because I know that God is in control. **Results:** I have a peace that certainly passes all my understanding.

- In 1991, after being a migraine sufferer most of my life, one Friday afternoon as I crawled down the hallway on my hands and knees to the bathroom in a school to find a dark place to loose my lunch and to find relief from the worst headache I had ever hand, as much as I could I cried out to the Lord that I belonged to him and that I believed Him when He said that He would never leave nor forsake me. I begged Him to please send His angels to help me...immediately, as I pushed open the door to the bathroom, I knew that he had sent someone to see me through. A wet cloth was administered to my head and the back of my neck was gently rubbed until the pain was released and I went fast asleep right there on the floor for a little while. I tried to believe it was another teacher in the building helping me, but of course I discovered that no one ever saw me crawling down the hallway. An angel, no doubt! **Results**: I know that He sends a comforter!

- The same year, after a move from one state to another for a position God certainly had opened the door for me to walk through, being without my family until school ended, I prayed that God would send me a friend to be with during this time of separation from my family. He did just that. For six weeks I had a best friend to play golf with, to study God's word with, to go to church with and to just minister to me. She and I saw each other every day of the week, several times during the day. We ate breakfast together, prayed together, had lunch and went to movies together. Long story short, when my family arrived I called this person to ask her to meet us for ice cream. She shared that she was busy so I told her I would call as soon as we returned. I tried to call her as soon as I returned to introduce her to my family, but the phone number I had used for months was now answered by a man who said he had been in the hotel room for months and that no one had ever been there. Even the folks we had seen daily as we golfed (our instructor, the hotel attendee, and others) did not remember seeing this lady! An angel...no doubt. **Results:** He gives us the desires of our heart.

- Several years ago, I broke my hip while traveling. As I laid in the rain asking God to be with me because cars were passing me on each side and water was splashing where it was difficult for people to see me, there was suddenly someone there beside me holding my hand and comforting me saying they would stay until someone arrived. We had a conversation (and I can't remember about what) but I remembered cars stopped driving by and I remembered that

the rain stopped immediately over me yet I could see the rain falling around me, and I had such peace. When the ambulance arrived, I looked around and the person was no longer there. I even asked the attendees if they saw a man standing near or walking away but no one saw a thing. And, even though it rained very hard, my clothing was not wet…nothing on me was wet! Go figure.
Results: God sends us a protector from harm!

- My last I'll share is about my brother who had been suffering with a heart condition for years. He had progressively gotten worse and had been told that he did not have a long time to live (I didn't know this as he kept it a secret). One night an angel came to my bed and whispered to me that everything would be alright, but to remember Lazarus, remember every detail, and then the angel left. The next morning I remembered this and prayed about it all day long. Later than night I received a call from my niece (my brother's daughter) that my brother had died around 11:00 pm. I immediately told her to go back inside, take my father's hand and to lay hands on my brother and speak his name to say "Leroy, wake up, in the name of Jesus" and to continue speaking it until he opened his eyes and responded, and assured her that all would be okay. Funny, I immediately hung the phone up (my husband said) and went fast asleep. The next day around 9am I called and was told that my brother had been pronounced dead but that he had come back alive again. I knew that God had sent me an angel to forewarn me to be aware and to speak the power of God into his life, that he would be given another chance to accept Jesus, an answer to my prayer and fulfillment of the promises God made to me. **Results:** God cares about our concerns, every one of them!

I can't begin to tell you how blessed I have been and continue to be to know that our God is an awesome God who provides us with everything we need, we only need to ask and to be obedient, and to believe, and to activate the power and His word in our life.

I am so grateful to be able to share these small tidbits that are very large in my life. I continue to pray that others will listen, learn and know that God is our Father who wants us to be the best we can be through Him and to give to each other through encouragement and assistance.

Finally, read this:

"Are not all angels ministering spirits sent to serve those who will inherit salvation?" Hebrews 1:14

God's blessings and strength to all who believe! Thank you for allowing me to share my stories.

Dr. Virginia Moody

Whatsoever Ye Shall Ask

There is a writing circling around that begins something like this, "People come into your life for a reason…" I am not sure of the reason that Taylor came into my life, but I remember well the day. It was a fall day and there was a noise in the hall of the school where I teach first grade. I went to investigate to find two middle school boys running and sliding down the hall on their knees. Because we had been having a problem with the kids playing in the hall after school, I firmly corrected them. One was not even supposed to be in the building, so I sent him on his way. When I asked the other young man his name, I met Taylor. Of course I explained to him that this was not a good choice and he needed to be a good example. Respectful and polite he was.

And that is how Taylor, his mom, and I met. For some reason, God had our paths cross. Through Taylor and his mom, my prayer life strengthened as I became more aware of the need to pray often and quietly. I learned that I can actually talk to God just as I talk to a person; He is everywhere. Taylor's faith, his outlook, his acceptance are light-years ahead of mine. His understanding of God's promises is just as God told us, childlike, that is, Taylor just accepts the promise without question, in faith.

Taylor's mom changed jobs and now we only communicate through email every now and then. Oddly enough, or is it, that when I receive those emails it has been at a time in my life when my faith or prayer life needs a jumpstart. As a matter of fact as I type this we have just been through some very long days with our miniature dachshund. I turned to the scripture Matthew 21:22, *"And all things, whatsoever ye shall ask in prayer, believing, ye shall receive."* On the floor, on my knees, I prayed and asked God to heal her, then I thanked God for healing her, and I opened my heart to receive her healing. Yes, she is a dog, but she is one of God's own creatures and some-times he sends the big creatures' messages through them.

And now, I pray for Taylor to be healed, and in my heart I receive his healing and each day I will thank God for his healing. For we as humans can not define healing by God's definitions.

Amelia Blaylock

Two Townhouses

There have been many times I have been sustained and moved forward with divine intervention. Sitting here answering letters, it suddenly dawned on me that we in these two town houses have just recently lived through an unbelievable miracle. For several years my niece Kay has suffered with problems arising from Raynaud's Syndrome. My sister Rose died, and her house, the townhouse adjoined to mine, was willed to my son Emil.

Emil decided that I needed company, so at the end of December my sister Lou and her daughter Kay (Emil's cousin) moved in. Within days, Kay was hunting for a new doctor, but she went to a foot doctor brand new here in the village. He sent her to a specialist in surgery and blood problems. This God-directed man tried to fix her left leg but by the time he got to it, it was dead. On the 17th of March he amputated her leg below the knee. This was not enough, so he had to go back to surgery and remove the leg about 3 inches above the knee.

Bless her sweet heart, she is doing wonderfully well. She is into her first prosthesis, she goes anywhere she wants go, either by wheel chair or the other leg, with which she is fast becoming comfortable. Yesterday she walked back and forth across the living-dining room area on her own! The prosthesis was in place, and Lou walked backward in front of her holding the walker if she should make a misstep. She's got the distance measured and has been using it as a track to do her practicing with the walker. When the therapist came today she really surprised him with her accomplishment! He was so pleased and told her that he had planned to start her walking alone next week.

Had the above listed series of events not occurred, with prayers from groups literally all over the world, and she had not moved here, and had the solid, unwavering support of her mother, Lou, she would be dead. Clearly, God intervened, and we are greatly blessed.

Elaine Hunziker

Angels Among Us

It was the spring of 2000. We had enjoyed a girl's vacation to Greece. It was me, my daughter, my sister and my niece. We had traveled all over the Greek Islands and were on the last part of our trip, in Athens, enjoying all the Greek history and learning about all the Greek gods.

We decided to spend our last afternoon doing some sightseeing. We got a taxi in front of our hotel and asked to be driven to a museum downtown. After touring through the museum we decided to walk toward the market area. We had a very crude map of the area and before long we realized we were lost. We decided after walking around in circles and trying to find the market area, we would just get a taxi and go back to the hotel. At this point we realized something unusual was happening. This was late afternoon when most people were getting off work and the buses and trains were on strike. Everyone was trying to get a taxi. People were doubling up in taxis and some were literally fighting for a taxi. Our situation seemed hopeless. We were too far to walk to our hotel so we continued to walk in the direction of the market hoping to get our bearings. We were four girl tourists standing on the sidewalk in downtown Athens, not knowing what to do next.

It has been nine years but I will never forget what happened next. If I were an artist, I could paint you a picture of the man that appeared before us. He spoke English, he was sixtyish, with gray hair, and he was well-dressed in a business suit. He asked if he could help us. We explained our problem. He raised his hand and waved and a taxi immediately appeared. Remember, there were none to be had. He became involved in an argument with the driver. The driver was going to charge a very high fare. All the drivers were taking advantage of the situation. Our benefactor continued to argue with him and told us to get in the taxi. He told us not to pay anymore than the customary rate which was $3.00. Our driver was not happy. He put the car in gear, we took off in a jolt, and we looked back but our angel had disappeared.

Scared and shaken, we arrived at our hotel. As we were standing there outside the lobby we looked at each other and said "Where did that man come from, and how did he disappear so quickly". We entered the hotel lobby and the hotel staff was warning everyone not to go to the market area because there were riots going on there. Angry with the USA for President Clinton's ordering of the bombing of Kosovo, the people were rioting in the streets. This is the direction we had been walking.

We all knew without a doubt that God had sent an angel to keep us from harm's way. There are truly angels among us.

Peggy Hopkins

Seeing the Beauty in God's Will

Spinal Muscular Atrophy, words I had never heard before, brought me to God, on my knees. Our first child, Spencer, was diagnosed at eleven months old, after months of fear, waiting, watching, willing him to bear weight on his legs, to roll over, to get to sitting. The milestones all parents watched for would not be celebrated. We were told Spencer would never walk, never stand, never play as other children do, and he would most likely succumb to respiratory illness very early in life. The grief and the heartache were unbearable. I felt I was mourning the death of a child. The future so carefully groomed in my mind was not to be.

My husband Kresten and I were both raised as Christians. We went to church together, taught Sunday school, and were active in the life of our congregation. I knew God. I knew Christ. I knew of the love and grace so freely given. But in all honesty, I had not given my heart to Christ. I was still fearful of the future, I still worried, and I tried to control events so the outcome would be my outcome. The outcome *I* felt was best.

I remember so vividly grieving in the quiet dark of our house for days; holding Spencer, praying that this diagnosis was wrong. Praying that our lives would go on as other families' lives did. Praying that God would give me a miracle. Gradually, I understood that I had to face our reality, the nightmare so many parents fear. Leaving our house, standing on the front porch, I found the world was not as I had left it. God's grace totally encapsulated me. I could feel the love and prayers lifted for us. God was tangible. He surrounded me. This was the first time that I knew my little family was not alone. We were being held in the palm of God's hand, and in the hearts of a very prayerful and loving community. And I knew we would be alright.

Twenty-one years later, I know my life and my family's lives have all been touched by this event. And what I had so vehemently prayed would go away, was God's plan for us. Once we accepted that, we could go on. I remember Kresten saying, "We will just have to make Spencer the best person we can, despite this disease." With that focus in mind, I was able to move forward. I have been able to accept God's plan for our lives, the easy and the difficult. What I have found is that God's plan for me has been richer than I ever could have hoped to dream - more than I knew to pray for.

Trevor was born four and a half years after Spencer. He is tall and strong, strong enough to lift his brother time and time again. He is gracious enough to kneel at his brother's feet to put on Spencer's shoes. He studies, he cooks, he wins photography awards, he somehow knows, at such a young age, that life is precious and every minute must be used, as Kresten always says, for adding value. Spencer and Trevor live in Austin together. Spencer is in his fifth year at UT's School of Architecture and Trevor will begin his first year. They take care of each other. This is an arrangement I could not have conceived of. If I had thought of it, I would have been praying for years. God's plans have been greater than my own imagination.

Accepting God's plan and learning to adapt, not to control, continues to be my goal. Soon after Spencer's birth, I learned the magazine I had been working for had gone bankrupt. Obviously a "bad" thing to happen at this time in our lives, but this event enabled me to move from advertising into education, something I had never considered until this time. Consequently, I have been given the opportunity to work with teachers, children, and families who are dealing with disability. My own experiences have made me compassionate and empathetic, but also a strong advocate for children. This was not a path I knew to follow. I still take a new step each day in the direction God has chosen for me.

Last year, I was diagnosed with Antiphospholipid antibody syndrome. Prior to the final blood test to confirm the diagnosis, I asked my renewal group to pray that the antibody was gone, which my doctor had already told me was highly unlikely, given that I had

had a deep vein thrombosis and confirmation of the antibody. My hematologist was surprised when the antibody was no longer detectable. She said,"Some things are just unexplainable." God's will is God's will, and prayer is powerful. We just have to be open to the answer, whether we like the answer or not. I have been given answers, many, many times. Often I know right away that I like the answer. In other cases, it is years later that I can see the beauty in God's plan, that I can see the visible results of what I had thought was an unanswered prayer.

I know without a doubt that my marriage is stronger; my relationships are deeper and more honest given the events in my life. I know Spencer is one of the strongest people that I know; he goes forward, touching the lives of those around him, expecting to encounter the world despite his disability. I know Trevor is a compassionate man - gentle, patient and driven to take every opportunity available to him, while adding value to the world. How much Kresten and I have learned together; I cannot begin to share the enormity of it.

But I know in my heart, that each event in our lives is an opportunity to glorify God. It is the love of Christ that brings us to our knees, that humbles us in the very vulnerability that pain and conflict bring.

Kimberly Cook

I Have the T-Shirt

One Saturday morning, several years ago, I got up early and got dressed to go to a Chamber of commerce meeting. It was very important to me since I was active in the community and promoting my business. I was hoping to meet some new prospects at the meeting as it was projected to have over 500 people there.

I was ready to go, and grabbing my purse with keys in hand when the "itch" on my hand became so intense it was like fire burning through my hand. I stopped at the back door. All of the sudden I was so over-whelmed with a sense of urgency to find my daughter. My heart was racing. I felt that she was in danger and I had to find her. The meeting was no longer important.

My daughter had run away from home several years prior to this time and I had no idea where she might be. I knew that she had lived in a particular apartment at one time and I had seen her at the bus stop directly across the street. The last job that I knew she had was downtown. I didn't even know if she was still working there. If she was still working there, I didn't know her schedule.

I was feeling weak all over. I got in the car and basically said, "God you have to tell me where to drive, I don't know where she is and you have to steer this car". I backed out of the driveway and decided to drive by the apartment complex and bus stop first.

I drove past the apartment complex and didn't see her. God was driving the car so I kept going and I drove down the street toward downtown very slowly and began to pray. I was so afraid; I started crying and praying, "Lord, please help me find her." I felt so lost and so alone. Is she alive or dead? I drove toward downtown looking in all directions to see if I could see her anywhere. I was looking between all of the old buildings as I drove down the street. They were all closed at this hour of the morning and it looked like a "ghost town".

I was driving down the street and felt that I should drive very slowly. My car was barely moving as I was looking on both sides of the street trying to find her. I was hoping she would be coming out of a building or see me driving down the street.

As I drove down the street, my heart started racing more and more and the sense of fear was over-whelming me. I felt I was getting closer and closer to her. I still couldn't see her and didn't know where she was.

I was getting closer and closer to the building where I knew she worked at one time and she was nowhere in sight. All of the sudden she saw me and walked out from behind some buildings on the left hand side of the street. She was shaking and white as a ghost. I asked her if she had time to get a cup of coffee and she got in the car.

On the way to get the coffee she told me that she was being followed by a man in a white van that kept circling around the block and he was trying to pick her up. She had hidden between some building hoping he would give up and move on.

After she told me about the van, I remembered that as she was coming out from between the buildings, there was a white van to my right. Apparently, I had driven between her and the white van. I thanked God, took her to work, and gave her to God again.

My daughter and I were very close until she became a teenager. When she turned 17 years old she decided to be on her own and left home with a girlfriend and fell into an evil world. After three heartbreaking days, she called to let me know she was alive and well but wanted to be independent and didn't want me to know how to get in touch with her. Over the next three to four years she would contact me periodically.

We are together again and we are rich with God's blessings. I thank God for saving her from the evil muck of this world.

For those of you who have suffered the loss of a run-a-way child…my heart goes out to you. "I have the "T-shirt" and know with God's help and earthly angels you will survive and God will bring more blessings to you than you can imagine. It will be God's timing and not yours.

Anonymous

Blessings & Thankfulness

I was raised in the United Methodist Church in California, but stopped attending the year before I graduated from high school. I was simply disinterested and quite frankly, didn't experience anything that had an impact on my heart. I stayed away from the church for the next 42 years, until I moved to Corpus Christi. Forty-two years, hum, that's longer than God kept the Israelites out of the Promised Land.

As a young woman, I studied classical voice and absolutely loved to sing. On Valentines Day in 1970, at age 22, I married my first husband, whom I had known for 2 years. Almost immediately, I knew something was wrong. I expected my husband to love and protect me and although he claimed to love me, he treated me with cruelty. There was no Oprah to set me straight. There was no one to protect me. In my mind, divorce was not an option. So, I remained in this marriage for seven years and gave birth to two daughters. We had moved back to Santa Barbara and bought a big 100 year-old Victorian house, my dream home. I had it all, and I had plenty of time to wonder just how I had ended up in this disastrous marriage.

The Marriage - For me, the worst was the mental and emotional havoc. I lost my smile, my voice, my love, my self-respect, my courage, my sense of adventure, my self-confidence, and most definitely, my sense of humor.

Finding Myself Again - Life was so desolate. I desperately needed freedom. My "light bulb moment" came in an unexpected way. I had sewn since I was nine years old and made most of my own and my daughters' clothes. The things I made were never good enough. One day, I was at the fabric store looking for an inexpensive remnant to make little dresses for my girls. I kept second-guessing my choices until I realized that I had been in the store for over an hour, trying to figure out which fabric I could choose that would cause the least amount of turmoil. It hit me like a ton of bricks. Why did I value my opinions so little? At that moment, I started pulling myself out of the misery. It took over a year to strengthen myself to a point where I could make the decision to ask my husband to leave. I remember the exact moment when I came to the realization that, if I got a divorce, my parents would still love me, and the world would go on turning. My heart had moved on with the hope of finding a better life. Jeremiah 29:11 *"For I know the plans I have for you, "declares the Lord," plans to prosper you and not to harm you, plans to give you hope and a future. "*

The Recovery - After the divorce, there was no time for fear or for self-doubt. I had two little sweethearts to tend to, on a pittance of child support, and my fierce determination. I worked my way up the career ladder to become a Comptroller for commercial construction companies. I remarried seven years later, in 1984.

THANKFULNESS - There are some things I know for sure. God has blessed me mightily and I thank him for his work in me.

God brought me to Corpus Christi and the First United Methodist Church. God put me in church service first, then Sunday School. My first day in Sunday School, Louella Wallace invited the women to the Corpus Christi Women's Bible Study. My acceptance of her invitation to participate in this Bible Study, has had a profound effect on my relationship with God and my happiness. God has blessed me with the friendships I have found there. Their open and heartfelt sharing is beyond my realm of experience. Because of them, I can readily and without questioning, accept and trust. They are my safe haven. Psalm 121:7 *"The Lord will keep you from all harm, he will watch over your life."*

*The 40 years that the Israelites <u>and</u> I were out wandering, I never asked God f*or anything. I had to be strong, rely on no one but myself. I felt it was wrong to ask God for anything, since I never thanked God for anything. I never gave him credit, nor did I blame him. Now, I know that by giving all the credit to God, and asking Him for His help, I have learned to ask and accept help from others. All of my worries do not rest solely on my shoulders. What a huge relief. God's grace has allowed His word and love to enhance my life immeasurably.

My music was the biggest aspect of my life that I didn't reclaim after my divorce. I still loved to sing, but it was a private thing, just for my girls, until it faded into a secret longing. God has given my music back to me, only in a way that I would never have imagined. It started the first time I walked into church and heard the band playing "Come Now Is the Time to Worship". I knew that I was in my right place. And now, I sing for God. Ephesians 5:19 *"Sing and make music in your heart to the Lord."*

I used to wonder; if not for my disastrous first marriage - What would I have been? Who would I have been? Now I know that I am exactly <u>where</u> God wants me to be and <u>who</u> God wants me to be. I wouldn't be the same person if I hadn't had to live the life I've led. I watch for and tend to the needs of others because I'll never forget the times when there was no one to help me. I no longer feel that God left me alone for all of those years, just that he stepped back to wait, until I turned to look for him. Psalm 138:3 *"When I called you, you answered me; you made me bold and stouthearted."*

The last thing I know is that I haven't accomplished everything that God has destined for me. I'm sure that there are many small tasks, but I believe that there is something bigger, and I look forward to seeing what God has in store for me. Ecclesiastes 3:1 *"To every thing there is a season, and a time to every purpose under the heaven."*

Dear Lord, I am thankful that for some, their journey to your grace has been shorter than mine. You blessed them with the Love of Christ at an earlier time in their lives. But I am grateful that you have made my journey longer, and that you have saved the "Best for Last".

Unsurpassed joy, abundant blessings, unending love, amazing grace... Amen

Anonymous

A Teacher's Test

I am currently retired after having taught freshman Biology for 31 years...and for the last nine years, Teen Leadership, a class which I continue to teach "in retirement" today. Old teachers never go away, do they?

This is a story of which I am not very proud. It is a story of turning a deaf ear to "a voice crying out in the wilderness." It is the story of a young man named Michael. Please rest assured that Michael has given me permission to use his name and to tell his/this story.

When Michael was in my Biology class several years ago, he hated me...he absolutely hated me, and to tell you the truth, I wasn't very fond of Michael. Michael was a "wannabe" gang member. He wore the colors...had the baggy clothes...flashed the signs...spoke the lingo.

I dreaded 5th period that year. Some days were so bad that when I would see Michael in the hallways in the morning, I was already dreading his eventual presence in my class, which was still FOUR hours away! He made my life a pure hell, and he enjoyed doing so. I thought perhaps things would get better as the year progressed, but they didn't. Day 177 was just as bad as day one. But the school year eventually ended, and I had SURVIVED! God put Michael in my life to "test" me, and I had passed the test. Or so I thought.

After reflecting that summer on what had transpired, I knew something was wrong. After all, I had always prided myself on the relationships I had with my students and student-athletes. Over the years, I had been asked (and had served) as Best Man twice, groomsman four times, and usher three times in the weddings of some of these kids.

What went wrong with Michael? Did God really put him in my life to make me miserable for a year? I survived, but was that what God wanted? The answer, of course, was "No." I had failed God's "real" test. He wanted more.

My friends, whenever God tests you and you fail, please know that He will test you again. Please know, too, that God has a sense of humor…

Two years later, guess whose name appeared on the roster of my Teen Leadership class? Yep, Michael's! I thought to myself, "Here we go again!"

Briefly, Teen Leadership is a one-semester course in which students learn to deal with life's issues. The class motto is: "What you see here…what you hear here…let it stay here when you leave here." The students learn to become vulnerable…transparent…and willing to trust their classmates. They are required to write in a journal and to give several speeches.

Michael? Trust? Take off the mask? Journal? Give speeches? Never! My hope (and prayer!) was that Michael, upon hearing of the class requirements, would run to the counselor's office to request a schedule change. He didn't. Thank God. Time and space do not allow me to reveal all that transpired that semester, but I do share with you now Michael's last journal entry. The assignment: "What has Teen Leadership meant to me?"

Coach Gorny,

Hey, what's up Gorny? I just wanted to say "thanks" for everything in this class.

It's been a good experience for me. I've never opened up like that before...I mean, you listened to me more than anyone.

I also wanted to say that I'm sorry for being such a pain in the @#*! But I also wanted to tell you that you've been like a father to me whether you knew it or not.

You know, my grandfather was the only father figure I ever had, and when he passed away, I just knew there would never be anyone to replace him in my life...until I met you.

My life is not perfect, but I live with it, and it's good to know I can talk to somebody. I am glad and very, very happy to call you my "father."

When you read this, I'll have only one more class with you...and hopefully, it will be my LAST class with you!

But all I wanted to say is that I'm sorry for having been such a pain and thanks for being there for me even on those days when I could not share/talk in this class. You were the only reason I gave my speeches.

So, as my last time writing in this journal, I thank you yet again...

Love...your son, Michael

Unbeknownst to me (all that time), Michael had been living in the prison of loneliness... despair... and hopelessness. His grandfather had passed away just before his freshman year... just before he had enrolled in my Biology class.

So, my friends, how did "hate" turn into love and understanding? Pretty easily, looking back now: (1) utilizing the techniques I had learned as a Table Leader on the Walk to Emmaus, (2) incorporating the "Four L's" of the Kairos prison ministry - Listen, listen, love, love, and (3) remembering that "a wise person hears one word but understands two."

Thanks for allowing me to share "our" story. Oh, by the way, Michael: (1) passed all his TAKS tests, (2) graduated from high school, (3) now serves his country in the U.S. Army Reserve, and (4) from what I've heard from friends, has received Jesus as his Lord and Savior. Amen!

Ed Gorny

Some time ago I counseled a young friend who is talking about separating from her husband after two years of marriage. It was a wonderful opportunity for me to tell about my faith, to someone who seemed to be struggling with hers. I have always felt inadequate in that regard and the Holy Spirit gave me the words to say to her. I pray that the seeds I planted with her will grow and be harvested as a rich faith base and the glue that holds her marriage together.

Dear XXXXX,

All day yesterday, I sent out prayers for you. This stuff is one of the hardest things to deal with, and we're usually so ill-equipped! At a time in our development that we've spent our entire existence being the center of our own universes, we're called to put someone else in that place - or at least it seems like that. And most of us just don't have the manual.

I'm glad to hear that the two of you don't want to give up, and that you've been in counseling, and that you're seeking to read what you can to help you get through this. Wish I could give you such wise words that you could just read them, snap your fingers, tell your husband, and happily go home together. If I had those, I could be a rich woman! But I will gladly share with you from my own experiences, and definitely from my heart, what I pray will be of some help.

It's quite a conundrum you're in. You don't want to leave your partner, but how do you stay together when you're "pouring gasoline" on each other? [They had watched the movie "Fireproof" and liked that allegory.] What's the gremlin that keeps biting you on the ankles?

Realizing that church and God haven't been a pivotal part of your life, I'm still going to share with you its importance in mine, because it's, well, important. Crucial. Essential. Too many years (and a couple of marriages) were wasted, or poorly spent, because I did not put God in the center of everything. My faith took YEARS to develop (and I'll never be finished with it), because my ego kept wanting to come out on top. And in marriage, just as in a relationship with God, fighting to stay on top will leave you in the dirt.

This marriage has taught me that lesson in painful fits and starts, because I have clung so stubbornly to my pride. It's been a struggle for him, too, as our life together reveals areas in which he sees he needs to grow and change. What has been our focal point, and it never fails when we manage it, is trying to be who God made us to be instead of the egocentric, prideful, short-tempered beasties we spent decades developing. And I'm not saying either of us has turned into a doormat - that's far from the truth! But I found a fragment of scripture that helps me when I least want to follow it: "Be blameless." When I feel I've been treated unfairly, and I'm having homicidal urges, that little phrase challenges me to rise above it. If I can act like Jesus would act, at least for a few seconds, not only can I avoid a few more flames (sometimes), but often I can help de-fuse a volatile situation. Most of the time I don't see immediate results, but there is always a reward somewhere in doing the right thing. And when you please God, He does bless you. Not like you can go to the God store and buy a few blessings with your good actions - but more like *the doing*, on your part, with your heart in the right place, is a blessing in itself.

Don't feed the fires, my friend. If you and your husband want to stay together, and want this to work, focus on staying together and making it work. All the peripheral stuff will fall in line if you make "the main thing the main thing." Over thinking can keep you very Unfocused, and keep you from doing the very thing you want to do. I know a separation sounds really attractive right now, but I sure wouldn't recommend it. It almost never builds a good marriage.

Okay, I'm already well into being preachy, and will try to step back a little - my finger's tired of wagging! I'll try some thoughts to help you through:

Seek to know God, and ask His help in everything.

Before reacting, "try on" being blameless.

When he is venting, put your own agenda aside and listen to him as if he were the only thing on earth that mattered (I need work on this one). You can ask him to do the same, but don't require it.

Acknowledge - often - that men and women were made very differently, and will never understand some things about one another. Then learn to be thankful (yikes!) for those differences.

Love each other. Then love each other.

Before my husband and I got married, he was so wounded and scared of another failed relationship. He said, "I know we're in love right now, but what happens when you wake up one day and the feeling's gone?" My answer (which is not easy, as you know) was, "That's when "love" becomes a verb." God is the author of love - that is WHAT He is - so without Him, that is, without relying on Him in our lives every day, our version of love will fall far short. Might as well go to the Expert!

Hope I haven't come across as flippant or insensitive. This subject is a painful one for me to address, for myself as well as those I care about, but it also brings me joy in the hope that is in it. I prayed for the words to share with you, so now I'm going to trust that the prayer was answered. I will keep praying for your hearts to be softened toward one another and for God to send His angels into your paths to help wherever you need it.

Anonymous

"Excerpt" of book entitled
Living It Up!

"It was the year 2000, and one of the toughest years my husband James and I have faced. We'd been married for four years and were thinking of starting a family. We began the New Year with James having a back injury and being unable to work. James' father was in the hospital, where he'd been since early December. Unexpectedly, his dad passed away on January 10th. James would continue to be in therapy and unable to work for five months. In February we found out that we were pregnant with our first child.

As we were deciding what girl and boy names to choose for the baby, I had an abnormal blood test come back. We soon found out that we were having a baby boy. We named him Jalen Uriah. We also found out that there could be 1-100 things wrong with him due to a rare condition called Mosaic Trisomy 16.

I became even more intentional in praying for our son. I typed every promise Scripture I could think of and passed them out to my family and friends and asked them to pray for a miracle with us. I prayed these Scriptures over my son every day! My tummy was getting bigger and bigger and I could even feel the baby moving at times.

James and I went to our twenty-week follow-up exam. I lay down as I normally did for the nurse to check the baby's heartbeat. The nurse moved the Doppler to the left and right, up and down. Nothing. She walked out of the room. James and I just looked at each other without saying a word. The doctor then came and told us that she wanted to do an ultrasound because the nurse couldn't find a heartbeat. Sure enough, through the ultrasound, James and I saw Jalen Uriah's little lifeless body in my womb. We were in shock.

I was admitted to the hospital early the next morning. Twenty-one hours later I gave birth to my stillborn son. Leaving the hospital empty handed was very surreal. I felt like a glass vase that had been dropped on a concrete floor and shattered into a thousand pieces. It was the hardest thing I have ever had to go through.

As if the loss of my husband's dad and our son wasn't enough, our year wasn't over. A month after our son's burial, I had surgery to remove a pre-cancerous mass from my Thyroid. James finally found another job, but with way less pay, so we continued struggling financially. Also, before the year was out, we both would visit the emergency room twice. Life had dealt us a hard year."

I am glad to say that is not the end our story. The Lord has since doubly blessed us with two boys, and has moved in wondrous ways in our lives. Being a believer doesn't mean that we'll never experience heartache, but it means that we have a God who is able, even in our darkest times, to bring healing, peace, hope and restoration. So in those seasons when you feel you can't trace Him, still trust Him. God is faithful!

Rochelle Roots

The Fixer

"Be Still My Heart…"

"Always" is how I answer the question, "When did you first learn about Jesus?" I always knew him. He was *always* in my heart. Growing up in a small community, we attended a country church that had beauty truly from within. Often drawn to a special place with my Lord by the hymns sung on Sundays, I felt His grace and love. In the late sixties, our family faced a tragedy that caused me to "stumble" in my faith. Back then, I did not realize that it was my faith in Jesus that was rocked and had been compromised. I knew that I had changed. My self-esteem: gone. My world as I knew it: vanished. Once an outgoing, popular young lady, I turned inward and decided to allow others to pass along ahead of me. My sisters and brothers, my friends and other family members…I was content to see them shine and prosper, while I became more and more vague and isolated. I was married at the young age of 18. Married, not for the same reasons most people marry. I married because I thought that it was the next logical step. I was out of my parents' house and into a new world of being a wife. Two children later, I found a new place to hide. I began to focus only on them and even less on me. At last, I found a way to fully disappear. I often felt belittled and unworthy during those days. So I prepared myself to *not* be an easy target. I immersed myself in the role of mother, denying myself thoughts of what I might need or want. Quietly, I toiled. And when the children needed new clothes or wanted to attend social events, the responsibility fell on me. I did whatever it took to allow them to never go without. Working two to three jobs, if need be, I did it. I became a "fixer." No one could get the things done like I did. My biggest success? Getting my son into and paying for his college career at Texas A&M University. No student loans. I did it. My son's father said at my son's graduation "Without your mother, this would have never happened." My children never went second-class; nor did they suffer. Nice cars, credit cards, fun money in their bank accounts, charge accounts at the dry cleaners; whatever they desired, I made it happen. Like I said, I was their "fixer." This role soon became the catalyst in my change. I decided I needed to "fix" me.

"Here I am Lord, I Heard You Calling in the Night."

I realized that by squashing myself and hiding, it was hurting me. I was pushing myself farther away from my Lord. And then it happened. When the children left home to find their own paths, it became very clear. Like losing my compass in a sand storm, I was gone. My body was there sitting across the kitchen table from my husband; but I was gone. My true spirit was lost somewhere in the past. I decided that I didn't want to live this way any longer. It was time to make a change. On my knees, I prayed to God for his governance. I prayed that He help me find myself lost long ago. I asked to be given a sign of what I should do. I needed to make a change. And I believed that the change would only happen if I left my husband and lived on my own. That is what I decided to do.

"Follow Me."

In spite of our earthly decisions, God uses what we do for His good. He spoke to me in a very loving and familiar language. He called to me in the language of music. Moment by moment, I had hymns of my youth placed in my head as they related to my pending journey. The strongest message was, "Follow Me." I was to follow Him from now on. I realized that which was missing in my life was not the spirit of my old self; rather it was my walk with God and my constant relationship with my Savior. Not completely without problems, my journey occurred, first creating a budget, then finding an apartment. God presented angels of mercy all around me so that each step was made with purpose and in the right direction. I grew confident as my journey progressed and more hymns came into focus. When I felt uncertain, I sang. When I felt scared, I sang; always singing, even if it was a "small" song, such as **"Jesus Loves Me."**. I was comforted by music.

"Then Sings My Soul"

Today my walk with God is evident and strong. As I have become anew, so my soul has been reborn. Fully rested and warmed by His word-made music, I am confident and happy to have made the journey. **"I am Thine, O' Lord, I have Heard Thy Voice."**

Vicki Pollard

God's Wallflower

I've recently spent a significant amount of time asking myself, "If I were to pass anything on to someone, a story or a word of advice, what would it be? What was a BIG lesson that I've learned in my life?" And so, I've done some filing and reorganizing of the mess that's in my head and, well, this is what I've come up with: Almost my whole life was spent as a wallflower. Hardly anyone ever noticed me in a room and those who did kind of just said, "Huh," and walked off. I was quiet and shy. A bookworm. A homebody. A nobody. I was all of the things that didn't equate to popularity. And for a long while, I was okay with that. I was happy with my life, my family and the friends that I did have. But one day when I was around the age of 10, I realized that things were changing around me and they were also changing the things inside of me. When my family life started falling apart, I started noticing a dark shadow beginning to encompass my mind. My family was constantly preoccupied with important matters that I was far too young to understand or appreciate and I began feeling neglected, overlooked and even rejected everywhere I went. The devil was constantly feeding me a load of negativity and so at that young age, I became depressed and borderline "psychotic". I began hearing voices and seeing images everywhere. I even made my first attempt at suicide by lying in the middle of the road late one night on a street with dim lights. I had appealed to my parents many times, telling them that I was hearing things or that I had really bad dreams that followed me around all the time, but they were too busy to trouble themselves with a little girl who read too many books and whose imagination was far too big for her to handle. And so I spent my pre-teen years alone in my room trying to fight off what I called my Black Box that would be my home for the bulk of my life; this Black Box that fed daily on my lack of self-esteem, self-worth and rejection constantly suffocated me from the inside out. During my school career, already enveloped by this Box, I made friends with cigarettes, drugs and alcohol. I stopped trusting people and gave up on relationships. Having been both molested and raped before the age of 20, I accepted that I would never be one of the lucky ones to experience love anyway. I had reached a point where not only was I an outsider among my schoolmates, friends and family, I felt like I was an outsider also in my own body. Even my antidepressants and antipsychotics couldn't quiet the demons in my head. Nothing could stop this darkness that was inside of me. My soul was in such turmoil that I had this constantly aggravating itch as if it was trying to claw its way out of my skin. My mind hurt from trying to make sense of it all. There was a poison inside of me and it was slowly infecting every inch of my being. At some point I started bleeding myself out hoping that I could expel at least some of the poison inside of me, if not all. And when that didn't work, I would overdose myself on prescription pills. I tried anything and everything to make the pain go away. All I prayed for each day was that God would have mercy on me and just let me die because I couldn't take it anymore. But he didn't. And so for many years, I continued to suffer from severe manic depression. I appealed to God on numerous occasions, even bargaining at times, but it was as if He wanted me to continue suffering. Even after He and I came to an agreement, that I just had to come to Him and He would take care of me, I continued to spend my nights in tears. I wondered and wondered why. Why must I suffer so much? Why couldn't He just take all the sadness away? Stop the hurt? Stop the memories? Show me what love felt like? Why did I always have to feel so alone and out of place? These questions continued in my mind but it was the first time that my thoughts cycled around God and not something else. I had always known God from church and my family, but I started looking deeper into who He was and what He wanted with me. I discovered His grace and His love, and I realized that He was with me and was suffering with me the entire time, and that He was just waiting for me to call on Him and to trust in Him. Jesus brought a peace to my heart that I had never known before. He released my asphyxiation from my Black Box and put a new breath in my lungs. In Jeremiah 29, He told me, *"I know the plans that I have for you, plans to prosper and not to harm you, plans to give you hope and a future. Then you will call upon me and come and pray to me, and I will listen to you..."* and He showed me a love that didn't waver even in the most tumultuous conditions.

Two years ago I discovered that I have an incurable disease, and that I am to simply suffer with it for the rest of my life. People approach me all of the time to talk about it and what I always say is, "Yeah, it stinks, but Christ said, 'My grace is sufficient for you, for my power is made perfect in weakness' and I know that He has everything in control if I just continue to trust in Him."

Emily Karim

A Faith Story

Several years ago, my husband (Larry), my daughter (Kimberly) and I were sitting in a hospital emergency waiting room, with three of Larry's five sisters. Earlier that evening we received a call telling us that Larry's Mom had a heart attack. While we were waiting for the doctors to tell us about her condition, a young couple covered in blood came in. They were immediately taken into the emergency restricted area. As it turned out, the young man was badly injured in a bar fight. The young woman kept walking in and out of the emergency room and I kept feeling a strong pull to speak with her. Every time I turned around I found myself face to face with her; I would walk out of the hospital and she would walk in. I would be walking in and she would be walking out. I remember thinking, "Lord, I don't know her, what would I say?"

At one point in the evening, some of us were sitting, but Larry, Kimberly and I were standing; leaning with our backs against the wall under the TV. The nurses' window and the door, to enter where the patients were being held, were to our right. The young woman came storming out and she threw her pass at the nurse, walked across the room and leaned against the wall directly across the room from me. I could resist no longer, the pull became a push; and although no one was behind me, I felt two hands on my shoulders pushing me toward her. I walked over and said something like, "I thought you might like someone to talk to." She told me that she and her husband were from out of State and they had come to Canyon Lake, Texas to get certified for diving. Afterwards they stopped in a pool hall to play pool and have a few drinks. That's where he got injured. She had no one else with her; she was alone.

I thought to myself, "Okay Lord, if you want me to talk with her, you have to open the door." As the thought crossed my mind, she reached over and picked up the Christian "fishy" on my necklace and asked, "What's this?" The door was opened and our conversation began. I explained to her that it was a Christian symbol, called an Ichthus, and it was used as a sign by early Christians to recognize each other when the early church was being persecuted. She looked at me in total surprise and said, "You're a Christian? Why are you at the hospital? I thought nothing bad happened to Christians." That took our conversation where God wanted it to go. I explained to her that life happens to all of us, that God never said we would not have problems. The difference is that when we face bad times, we never have to face them alone. Jesus is always with us. God loves us, carries us through the difficult times and we are never alone. Then I understood why I was there. I reached up, removed my necklace and put it around her neck. She protested, but I told her, "God wants you to know that you are not alone. I didn't want to come over here and talk to you; I was afraid, but God insisted. He wants you to know that He loves you and He is here." I asked her if she had ever seen the picture of Jesus standing at the door knocking. She said yes, but she didn't understand it. I told her that Jesus is knocking for us to let Him in. There is no door knob on His side of the door. God is always with us; we are never alone. All we have to do is open the door and let Him in.

Our conversation turned back to her current situation. I looked over at Larry and he and Kimberly instinctively came over. I introduced them and he gave her money for the pay phone. As she turned to call home, the doctors finally called our family into a separate room. She didn't want me to leave, but I told her I would be back. In time my mother-in-law would be fine and she even stopped smoking because of her scare; another answered prayer. I never saw the young woman again, even though I anxiously looked for her as we left. I have often wondered about the seed that was planted in her heart that day, but my heart told me that I had done what I was supposed to do. When we got home, Kimberly gave me her Ichthus necklace that matched mine. I protested, but she wanted me to have it.

Trish Scharmann

The Most Unforgettable Year, 2006

Every February, my husband and I always go on a trip for our anniversary. The year 2006 was special because we were going to be celebrating our 10-year anniversary. We decided we would go on a cruise because we had been on one for our honeymoon. Our ship sailed Sunday afternoon. Early Monday morning, I woke up to hit the gym. Towards the end of my workout my husband came to get me. He asked me to come to the room right away. In the past, he would surprise me with an anniversary gift of some kind so I thought nothing of his request. Once we were in the room, he told me that my brother called. That was weird; the only way to receive a call is by ship satellite. My husband told me that my Dad had passed away. I could not believe what I was hearing. I hoped it was a joke, but who would joke like that? His face said it all; he was not joking. Well, as you can imagine, I was in shock. We immediately went to see about getting off the boat.

We would have to wait to disembark at our first port and that day would be Wednesday. We were able to make calls and prepare to return home. Follow this timeline: Embark Sunday, notified Monday, first port Wednesday and travel all day, rosary for my dad on Thursday and burial Friday. What an exhausting week. During the waiting period, I had the opportunity to write some thoughts down to give a little talk about my dad Thursday night. He always talked about how he was ready to be with the Lord. He would actually pray for it. I miss him dearly. After all was said and done, I held my mother and asked her not to leave me anytime soon. I really needed her. Taking your family for granted was a wake up call for me.

I used to ride my bike for 20 to 30 miles everyday. One day, while on my ride, my older sister called me to notify me that our mother had passed away. Once again, shock trembled through my body. Are you sure? My sister would not joke about that. We had just buried my dad 60 days ago. My mother had been diagnosed with stage 1 breast cancer the year before. She went through a mastectomy and chemotherapy. Since it was diagnosed at such an early stage, she was done with treatments in six months. She had beaten it. Right before her passing, she was advised of a leaking heart valve. The day she was scheduled to see the doctor after a spell, she passed while getting ready for her appointment. Funeral arrangements, again. The last letter my mother had written to me was regarding my spiritual growth. I read that letter at her rosary. I was not prepared for her passing. I miss her dearly, too.

Thanksgiving had come and gone. I was on my way home for lunch one workday and my husband called me to notify me his dad had died. There is no way! Three parents in the same year? I was in a complete state of shock, again. What made this one even harder to bear is that he took his own life. He and his wife had been going through some hard relational times. We were so taken back by this. His death was untimely because he was healthy, but obviously he was not in a normal state of mind. We had questions. Will we be with him in heaven? I contacted our pastor and he reminded us that God's grace and mercy is powerful. The worst of the worst can get into heaven as long as they sincerely ask Jesus into their hearts and accept him as their Lord and Savior. My husband's dad had done that, so knowing that relieves us. My husband and I had to make arrangements to travel out of the state to attend yet another funeral. It was so sad for us. At this point, what was next?

Why did this happen to me? Why not? Many people lose their parents in this manner or at the same time for that matter. I grieved, questioned, got really mad, and at times a bit of depression would set in.

I do believe that if your heart is right with God, understanding and acceptance comes quickly. Healing is rapid. Plus, our parents loved God and all three of them had accepted Jesus Christ as their personal Savior, so I know that I will join them in

Heaven forever. That keeps me going, in addition to the memories I hold in my heart.

Love the people who surround you: grandparents, parents, spouses, sisters, brothers, aunts, uncles, cousins, children, grandchildren, co-workers, neighbors, and even your pets. One day they will be gone and if you remind them now of how much you love them, they will love you back. Do not take anyone for granted, for that is the saddest thing. One last thought, love God first with all your heart and the rest will come easy.

I dedicate this memory to my husband, sisters and brother.

Bill. Clara, Denise, Maurice, and Maria (Gina)

In loving memory of

Willie Rodriguez
Gloria R Gutierrez
Virgil Koch

God Bless You and I Love You,

Grace Koch

Twist, Turns and Rocky Roads

For 35 years it was always a place we went for rest and relaxation. A little house in the mountains was the place we called our vacation for so many years. Surrounded by the snow-capped mountains, with the rivers and streams rushing by, and the wildflowers with their vibrant colors, it was not hard to realize that God made this glorious part of the Earth.

But this year was different. For the first time I went to spend time in this piece of my heaven as a single person. The past 4 years have been difficult. We sent our last child to college, packed up our home of 19 years and moved to a new town hours from family and friends. Two years later a divorce; continual court hearings dragging out the process; my move alone to a new town in which to heal; and the search for a job in the worst economy in many years. My faith had grown; I knew that God was with me on this journey. He had led me to find an apartment where I found safety and peace. He led me to find a place to call my church home where I felt His presence every time I walked through the doors or even drove by and saw the tall bell tower reaching towards the heavens. He sent His earthly angels to cross my path when I was depressed about not finding a job, about being alone, about my failed marriage.

And now without a job prospect and running short of money, my mother wanted to go to Colorado—a girls' trip with my sister and me to my place of paradise. The Texas summer had been scorching, so a respite from the heat was enticing. My mother offered to pay for part of my plane ticket, but I did not know if I could go. Could I face the room where we moved the bed out to the porch and lay under piles of quilts, watching the stars? Could I find my way to the lakes and rivers that we had been to so many times before to hike and fish? Could I face the memories? I committed to the trip, thinking that I would get a job and would not have to go to face my fears. When the time came, I did not have a job, so I went.

We spent the first few days in the mountains just being: reading, listening to the songs of the birds, looking at the glorious landscape of snow-topped mountains and the cozy little town sitting in the valley below. I took a glorious hike through mountains and wildflower fields, gently walking across the streams that ran from high on the mountains. My sister and I walked through the little mining town, stopping to talk with the locals. But through these adventures my mother stayed behind. The arthritis in her back kept her from hikes or even walking very much. She did not complain, just enjoyed the beauty that surrounded us.

After a few days I knew that it was time to take Mom for a drive to see the wildflowers in the valleys, to see the streams with the fishermen on their banks so gently and gracefully casting their lines, and to find the beautiful lake where my family and I had marveled in past years. Off we went on the gravel road. The road soon became a dirt road. The sign said 4-wheel drive only. We did not have a 4-wheel drive car, but we continued on the road a little longer. The road changed from packed dirt to a narrow path with potholes and rocks, twists and turns, but we continued to drive. The curves were so tight on the road, so narrow, that we could not see around the curve, and only one car could fit on the road which was next to a cliff headed down the high mountain pass.

My feet were sweating. Mom suggested turning around. I said one more curve...and then one more... and then one more. Thank you, God that we made it around another turn and did not meet another car. One more curve. I wanted to turn around. I wanted to go forward.

And there it was. We were looking down on the most glorious of mountain lakes, fed only by the streams of melting snow, tucked away in the high valley where it often spends the summer surrounded by the winter snow. We were here thanking God for his delivering us safely to the lake surrounded by spring wildflowers, thanking God for this beauty He put before us. Thanking God that my mother could visit this place and be among the wildflowers placed at our feet.

On the return trip, I congratulated myself for the bravery in making the drive, for the fortitude of not turning around, of going forward to my goal. It struck me! It wasn't me who went out on my own to find this lake…it was God's leading. God had a lesson for me to learn that afternoon.

As it is in life, it is God who leads us. With us not knowing what lies ahead on the twists and turns of the rocky road in life, it is God who stays next to us. It is God who nudges us not to return to the safety and security we perceive is waiting for us. It is in forging ahead with faith that we receive the most beautiful of gifts-God's gift for us.

And so it is with my life. I am continuing to go forward. I am continuing to trust in God's leading me around the twists and turns on the potted out roads; continuing to that glorious peace that is waiting somewhere up ahead.

Rebecca Maxfield Brindley

Delight yourself in the Lord, and he will give you the desires of your heart. Psalm 37:4:

I grew up in Indonesia as the daughter of Baptist missionaries. When I was a child, I would awaken every morning before sunrise by the sound of the morning prayers from the neighborhood mosque. I heard Moslem prayers 5 times a day for 10 years of my childhood. After the sun came up, my mother would frequently come into my bedroom and wake me up with another song: Hari ini, harinya Tuhan, Mari kita bersukaria which comes from Psalms 118:24 and translates into "This is the day that the Lord has made, Let us rejoice and be glad in it!"

I am blessed beyond measure to have been raised in a Christian home, with loving, praying parents who answered God's calling in their lives and instilled faith in their children. As a child, I had the added blessing of being surrounded by music every day. Music was as much a part of our home as the furniture. Some of my happiest childhood memories are of singing around the piano as a family while my father played. As a child, I thought all families spent their free time singing in harmony around the piano.

I started taking piano lessons when I was 8 years old. Piano lessons were not optional. When I was 17 years old and a junior at the Jakarta International School in Jakarta, Indonesia, my Chinese piano teacher "fired me" as a student for not practicing enough. She accused me of being more interested in boys than in my piano lessons. At the time, I didn't know a piano teacher could or would fire a student, but she was right—I *was* more interested in boys than in the piano. At 17, I was relieved that my teacher gave me a legitimate excuse for no longer practicing, but the deep desire to play the piano remained in my heart.

After my piano teacher fired me in Jakarta, Indonesia, I didn't play the piano again for 26 years. During those years, I sang in various musical groups—such as my church choir, theatre ensembles, even a small bluegrass trio, but I lacked the confidence, courage and time to practice the piano. I was too busy with motherhood, marriage, and a stressful career to think about the desires of my heart.

In 2001, I was shocked and horrified to find my marriage, full of hope and promise and 2 young sons, unraveling right before my eyes. I felt helpless and ill-equipped to deal with the breakdown of my marriage. As a child, I only knew one missionary couple in Indonesia who got divorced and it was very scandalous and shameful. To make matters worse, my parents were in Indonesia at the time and I was alone in Corpus Christi, Texas with no family, except my two young sons. I felt so much shame; I couldn't even bring myself to go to church. Seeing all the couples and families sitting together in the sanctuary broke my heart and added to my pain and feelings of failure.

It was during this time of brokenness—when my spirit was crushed and all I could do was get on my knees and beg God for mercy and forgiveness—that I finally understood the meaning of all the scriptures and hymns I'd memorized as a child. God, in His grace, mercy, and compassion, knelt down beside me, and carried me in His arms. Over time (not overnight), I experienced that peace that Paul talks about in Philippians—the peace that passeth all understanding. Despite the chaos, the suffering, and the great ache in the depths of my soul from my broken marriage and spirit, I knew for certain that I was not alone—God was with me, my children, and our family. For the first time in my life, I could relate to Paul's words in Romans 5:3-5: "…*but we also rejoice in our sufferings, because we know that suffering produces perseverance, perseverance, character, and character—hope. And hope does not disappoint us, because God has poured out his love into our hearts by the Holy Spirit, whom he has given us.*"

Several years after my divorce, when I was still in the process of healing, I was asked by some parents and teachers at Incarnate Word Academy, the Catholic school where my sons attended, if I would be willing to lead the weekly Mass music at the Middle School level. I was told the children were not participating in the music and I was asked to introduce more upbeat, contemporary worship songs to the Mass, in hopes that the children would sing and participate more. For the first time, I felt a strong calling from God that I should agree to help, but I had doubts and kept saying to myself—*I can't do this! First of all, I'm not Catholic—I don't know the Mass parts and I don't know when to sing, when to kneel, when to stand. I don't even play an instrument. All I have is my voice. How can I lead a Catholic congregation (even Middle school kids!) in music when the only hymns I know are Baptist ones?* Yet despite my reservations, I continued to feel called. I still felt shame about my divorce and I was surprised that the Catholic Sisters and teachers would even want a divorced, Protestant woman to lead the music at a Catholic Mass—even at the Middle School level!

About this time, I was leading the music on a Walk to Emmaus retreat, and one of the spiritual directors said—*If God is calling you to do something and you don't feel equipped to do it—accept the call in faith and know that God will equip you and will bring someone to help you. God doesn't call the equipped—he equips the called.* On the weekend of that retreat, I claimed this promise, stepped out in faith, and agreed to lead the music at the school, despite my insecurities. Before school started, God sent a wonderful, Catholic man—a leader in the community—with the most giving, gentle spirit, to help me with the music. He faithfully came to the school every week for 6 years with his guitar in hand to help me with the music and he knew all the Mass parts.

One of the parents at the school donated an outdated CASIO keyboard to our little Mass choir and after 26 years, I started playing the piano again. It was the perfect setting for me to take initial steps towards realizing my lifelong dream—as a congregation made up of 6th, 7th, and 8th graders is very forgiving. They didn't judge me or criticize me when I hit a bad note—in fact, they barely noticed! To my complete surprise, after a lot of hard work and hundreds of hours of practice, I discovered that I could play the piano by ear. I'd never taken the time or made the effort to explore this God-given talent in the past. Even my own parents were amazed.

Several years later, one of the Sisters at the school wrote me a kind, encouraging note that I keep on my piano to this day: *Dear Cheri, You have awakened in our school community a real joy in praising God in song—a joy that spills over into other areas. I love hearing the students, especially the boys, humming or singing one of the songs we've learned as they go from class to class.*"

When I gave my talents to God and answered His call, he gave me the great desire of my heart—to play the piano and write music. In 2005, I wrote my first song—a song for my grandparents. Afterwards, my Dad said to me—*Cheri, you've written one song and now you can write another*. He was right! I feel God gave me the ability to write music at this particular time in my life to give voice to what was in the depths of my heart and in the hearts of others who had suffered. As I began to write music, I studied the lyrics and chord structures of my favorite hymns from childhood. To my surprise, some of my very favorite hymns were written by women, like me, hundreds of years ago with their own stories and hurts and triumphs. I also discovered that most of the old hymns either directly or indirectly reference scripture and I believe that's the secret to the hymn's lasting influence from generation to generation. A composition teacher once told me that he hears bits and pieces of old hymns in the songs I write today. Yes, I've been influenced by the hymns I sang as a child in the Baptist church in Indonesia. They are part of my heritage—part of my faith journey—and they have comforted me my whole life.

The hours I now gladly spend at my piano are like going into a closet and praying—it's my own quiet time with the Lord where he speaks to me through the music he gives me, and it is awesome. I feel the music God gives me is healing music that is intended to strengthen and comfort others. I feel privileged to have been given the gift of music, and I feel it is my responsibility to share the gift with others as God leads and calls for His glory and purposes, for *"we have different gifts, according to the grace given us"* Romans 12:6. I am living proof that when we delight ourselves in the Lord, step out in faith, and follow God's call to use our gifts, He gives us the desires of our heart when we least expect and deserve it.

On Easter Sunday, 2008, I had the privilege of witnessing Taylor Berry's baptism. Taylor asked to be baptized on Easter Sunday and his own father baptized Taylor and his sister, Aubrey, in Kingsville Texas. The following song, ***Child, You're Not Alone***, was inspired by Taylor and his mother, Tamara.

Cheri Milam Roman

<u>Child, You're Not Alone</u>
Words and Music by Cheri Milam Roman and Holy Scripture
Written 8/9/08-8/10/08, 9/27/08, and 8/14-16, 2009
Dedicated to Taylor Berry and his mother, Tamara, and to Sister Eileen, in deep appreciation for her life and her support of my music, and to the very ill young woman who I saw walking into Spohn Hospital on October 2, 2008 holding the hands of two Sisters.
Verse 1
When your heart is breaking *(Psalm 73:26: My flesh and my heart may fail, but God is the strength of my heart and my portion forever.)*
And your eyes grow weak with tears- *(Psalm 31:9: Be merciful to me, O Lord, for I am in distress; my eyes grow weak with sorrow, my soul and my body with grief.)*
Don't be afraid! *(Matthew 14:27: But Jesus immediately said to them: Take courage! It is I. Don't be afraid.")*

I'll never leave! *(Hebrews 13:5-6: ..because God has said: Never will I leave you; never will I forsake you. So we say with confidence, The Lord is my helper: I will not be afraid.").*

I'll help you persevere *(Matthew 10:22 ...but he who stays firm to the end will be saved.).*

Pre-chorus

I won't give you more *(I Corinthians 10:13: No temptation has seized you except what is common to man. And God is faithful; he will not let you be tempted beyond what you can bear. But when you are tempted, he will also provide a way out so that you can stand up under it.)*

Than you can bear *(Psalm 145:14-16 The Lord sustains all who fall, And raises up all who are bowed down.)*

My promise is true! *(2 Corinthians 1:21: Now it is God who makes both us and you stand firm in Christ. He anointed us, set his seal of ownership on us, and put his Spirit in our hearts as a deposit, guaranteeing what is to come.)*

Just give me your cross *(Matthew 11:28-30: Come to me, all you who are weary and burdened, and I will give you rest. Take my yoke upon you and learn from me, for I am gentle and humble in heart, and you will find rest for your souls. For my yoke is easy and my burden is light.)*

Let me carry it for you.

Chorus

You're not alone—Look up! I'm standing here! *(Psalm 121:1 I lift up my eyes to the hills-where does my help come from? My help comes from the Lord,* *the Maker of heaven and earth; I Chronicles16:11: Look to the Lord and His strength, seek His face always)*

Through the terror of the night *(Psalm 91:5: You will not be afraid of the terror of the night, nor the arrow that flies by day).*

I'll draw you near *(James 4:8 Draw near to God and he will draw near to you.)*

You're not alone—It's my voice you hear! *(Hebrews 3:7: So, as the Holy Spirit says: Today, if you hear His voice, do not harden your hearts.")*

In the dark, I'll lift you up. *(Psalm 139: 12: Even the darkness will not be dark to you; the night will shine like the day, for darkness is as light to you. Psalm 91: 11 For He will command his angels concerning you to guard you in all your ways; they will lift you up in their hands. James 4:10 Humble yourselves in the sight of the Lord, and he shall lift you up).*

I'll hold your fear *(2 Timothy 1:7: For God has not given us a spirit of fear, but of power and of love and of a sound mind. Isaiah 41:10: Do not fear, for I am with you; Do not anxiously look about you, for I am your God I will strengthen you, surely I will help you, Surely I will uphold you with My righteous right hand.).*

Child, You're not alone!

Verse 2
And in your weakness,
You'll find you will be strong *(2 Corinthians 12:10: That is why for Christ's sake, I delight in weaknesses,*

in insults, in hardships, in persecutions, in difficulties. For when I am weak, then I am strong).
Don't be afraid! I'll never leave.
I'll stay beside you all night long. *(Psalm 121: 3-6: He will not let you foot slip—He who watches over you will not slumber: indeed, He who watches over Israel will neither slumber nor sleep. The Lord watches over you—the Lord is your shade at your right hand: the sun will not harm you by day, nor the moon by night.)*
PRE-CHORUS TO END

Cheri Milam Roman

Child, You're Not Alone can be downloaded from my myspace page www.myspace.com/cherimilamroman

Faith & Hope

The day I found out I was carrying twins was one of the happiest days of my life. No words can describe the happiness of my family. At 16 weeks a routine ultrasound was performed but was not good news. Twin A had developed a cyst on the back of her head that ran down her spine. The diagnosis was cystic hygroma. The doctors and the fetal experts did not give us much hope. My heart was so sad I was not sure I could get through this. Both were girls, I knew right away that twin A would be named Faith and twin B would be named Hope. On February 8th 2000, also my Father's birthday, Faith Rutherford arrived still-born. By God's grace, my womb completely closed, enabling me to continue the pregnancy for the second twin. Eighteen days later, February 26th, 2000, Hope Amber Rutherford was born weighing only 2 lbs 1 ounce. After two months in the NICU unit Hope arrived home.

God gave me Faith for a time, and now I have Hope everyday.

Susan Rutherford

Friend of God

2 Corinthians 5:18 says, *"All this is from God who reconciled us to himself through Christ and gave us the ministry of reconciliation"*

When my friend Tamara discovered that her son Taylor needed a heart transplant, she, Taylor, and her one-year-old daughter were forced to leave Corpus Christi and move to Houston to be nearer to the transplant team at Texas Children's Hospital. We helped move her to Houston into a one-bedroom apartment near the hospital in a relatively poor section of the City. I will never forget the look of loneliness on the faces of those three as we drove away and left them to come back to Corpus Christi. During the next six months before the transplant she and the children were virtually confined to the walls of that little one-bedroom apartment trying to keep Taylor healthy while they patiently waited on a heart. As often as I could, I would make trips to visit with them, sometimes to relieve my friend of some of her day-to-day duties and to allow her time to get away, if only briefly, and sometimes just to hang out and spend time with the three of them. Because of their confinement and the limitation of being around crowds, they had not been able to be in church in some time. So, one weekend while I was in Houston, we decided we would "do church" for the kids that Sunday morning. So, sitting in our pajamas in the living room, we studied the scriptures in the New Testament of Jesus leading his disciples to catch a boatload of fish and telling them to be fishers of men. We drew and cut out paper fish, and we strung those fish all around that little apartment! We had a blast! But the BEST thing was what happened next. There was a Russian family that lived in the apartment complex that had a little boy just about the same age as my friend Taylor. This little guy barely spoke any English. Occasionally Taylor and this child would play outside in the courtyard of the apartment complex. Well, later that Sunday afternoon, we found Taylor sitting outside in the courtyard with his little Russian friend, telling him all about Jesus, the boatload of fish, and being a fisher of men!

May we, Lord, have the enthusiasm of a little child to help our friends become friends of Christ.

Pam Teel

Plain Vanilla

My testimony would have to be one that many would describe as plain vanilla. I have never felt it was remarkable enough to capture for other's benefit. I have lived a fairly unremarkable life. Born in 1960, I grew up in Houston, Texas in a typical middle-income, Christian family with three kids, . I attended church most Sundays and a lot on Wednesday nights, singing in the choir, going to summer camp, playing football on the church team, and actively participating in the youth group as a teen. My dad's father was a Methodist minister. Unfortunately, I did not have the joy of knowing him, as he and my grandmother were killed in a car wreck long before my parents met. My maternal grandparents played a very active role in my childhood, and in the development of my faith. Christ was always a part of my life.

As a teen, I was active in youth fellowship at another church with more evangelical roots. Through it I heard for the first time about accepting Christ as my Savior and asking Him into my heart. I would listen to people give their testimony and talk about the wonderful epiphany they had when they asked Christ into their lives; how they could literally feel a change come over them when He entered. Several of these times I followed the instructions offered and asked Christ to come into my heart, but never did I feel any different. Maybe I should restate that. I felt shame and fear. Did Christ not want to come into my life? Was I not worthy of His love? Did He not want me? Had I been rejected?

The last time one of these 'rejections' occurred was on a retreat in East Texas. I remember the hall in which we were gathered like it was yesterday. A man had given a very moving testimony about his life as a hard-charging biker and how Christ had changed his life, how he had felt this wonderful feeling come over him when he accepted Christ as his savior. At the end of his presentation they asked us to pray, and for those who chose to, to accept Christ. I did it, again, as honestly and sincerely as I could. Afterwards, I felt no different.

The meeting broke for the evening and we all headed to bed. I felt miserable and the feeling kept getting worse until I was finally crying. I sought out the leader of the trip, finding him in his bed. Tearfully I told him what had happened this evening and at other times. He kindly put his arm around me, giving me a loving and accepting hug. He assured me that not everyone feels this great epiphany, particularly people who have grown up knowing Christ from an early age. He told me that Christ had been with me for a long time. That night, for me, was an affirmation more than a conversion. A smile and a great feeling of comfort quickly replaced my tears. I thanked him profusely and returned to bed, sleeping in comfort knowing that Christ had not rejected me.

I have been blessed to have Christ in my life. I have faced minor challenges throughout, but have always taken comfort that God was there for me. He has been the only constant that I could turn to for strength. He has blessed me with great health, a wonderful wife, and two fantastic daughters. I know He is watching over me and I take great comfort in that knowledge.

And, I am having the worst year of my entire life. Due to changes in the economic scene, my wife's job, and earnings, has gone to nothing. She is distraught about what the future looks like for her as a real estate investment banker. I have lost several business deals that were just at the edge of closing. And, like many others, our investments have been reduced so dramatically that I do not want to know what percentage of decline I have suffered in my principal.

We are having to sell our vacation dream home in Austin, the place I envisioned as a retreat for us, and particularly my daughters and their friends as they go through their teens. We have downsized a car, sold our boat, and are currently lining up other items to liquidate. Back in the fall, we bought a wonderful home that we may also have to sell. We got a dog that has more energy than my wife and young children anticipated, and at times they come to me crying. All this is putting an obvious strain on our marriage. Then, I have greatly compounded this strain by not being truthful to my wife about some of my behaviors. Now my marriage is threatened. I do not know where it will all end up.

But I do know that God is with me. In some of the darkest times this year I can see His hand at work. Additionally, He has brought me several good Christian friends in whom I can confide. I realize that in many parts of my life I have surrendered to God, but in a few aspects I have held on to my way. I believe this year is about Him showing me my failings. I am having to look at myself and ask "What kind of man will I be in this next stage of my life?" He is helping me to see my weaknesses with the brightest of lights. It is uncomfortable and painful. He is showing me that the material items and money are not mine, but His.

I am learning to fully surrender to Him. I know He is there for me, and always will be.

Anonymous

Dear Terri,

Thank you for allowing me to be a part of the "journey" in your awesome development of the book of testimonies. There are so many blessings associated with it. In my situation, I was blessed with the inspiration of the painting. I was lying in bed watching TV one evening, getting ready to go to sleep, when I had the inspiration to paint. I quickly picked up and old painting I had done, flipped it over, and starting painting. I have tried several times to do another painting like the original one and have not been able to accomplish it. This apparently was a one time event, done for a special purpose, by the grace of God.

The experience of talking to people about contributing stories to the book has also been a wonderful journey. It has opened doors that never would have been opened. I have been able to connect to fellow Christians that I didn't know where Christians before I presented information about the book.

God introduced me to "future Christians" and God led me to a place that I felt His presence.

Our God is an awesome God. May you and the Berry Foundation continue to be blessed by His awesome grace.

Love,

Sylvia Ramsey

12 - 6 - 10

Blessings,

Sylvia Ramsey

Outrageous Living

Several years ago my aunt sent a card congratulating me on my retirement. It had four women on the front in large coats with the largest most outlandish hats I had ever seen. The caption at the bottom said, "My goal is to do something outrageous everyday." I thought it very fitting as I headed into this new phase of my life.

Soon after retirement I began to plan for a mission trip to Uganda, Africa. For several weeks I had been preparing for teaching and leadership training. I kept thinking how this was a big step of faith for me, but God equips those he chooses, right? Well, almost immediately after I signed up for the trip I began to have anxiety attacks about being on a plane for so many hours. I would just rather be strapped to the wing, if I had a choice. I'm claustrophobic. For weeks this went on and finally, God was faithful and gave me Matthew 8:26 where Jesus tells his disciples *"You of little faith, why are you so afraid."* Well, it was a moment for me, kind of a "duh" moment, if you really want to know. God telling me just like the Twelve, "How much more do you need to see to believe?"

Well, I was much calmer in the following weeks, but Satan continued to pound on my psyche. I began to be fearful of the weirdest of things. Really, there were too many to mention, but they were all completely groundless. As the days grew closer, I prayed harder, and God continued to reveal His grace to me. Do you know that there are 366 scriptures on fear! One for everyday of the year plus one for leap year! I got His message from Scripture, from my own prayer time, from others praying for me, from the book we were reading in Sunday school, from a poem on my refrigerator, even from cleaning out my purse, and on and on.

What I came away with is this. If I had not agreed to be called to Uganda, I would not have been fearful. I was way out of my boat. If I had not been scared of going where I felt called, I would not have reached out to God and received so much. Really, I was overwhelmed with His encouragement. Then as I processed all this I realized that God wants us to wake up each day with this same scenario. What if we woke up every morning and in our minds we tried to imagine the wildest, scariest thing that God would call us to do that day. We would feel inferior, unequipped and overwhelmed with fear. We would be driven to His Word, driven to prayer, driven to other Christians for encouragement so that we might see more clearly how God wants to use us. He wants us to get up everyday and say, "OK Lord, what will you have me do today that is OUTRAGEOUS!!"

I say embrace the fear! If you don't get out of the boat, you won't be able to walk on water! I'm learning to love the thrill and God continues to press and stretch me.

Terri Shook

Passing from Life to Death

Me: *"Grandma, why did my mommy and daddy get divorced?"*

Grandma: *"It just didn't work out, Glen."*

Me: *"Well, why do I get to live with you while Mommy works?"*

Grandma: *"She has to work to make a living. You would have to stay with a babysitter in Ft. Worth if you lived with her. This way, she can work and know you are being taken care of by people who love you. Why? Do you want to live with your mama?"*

Me: *"No, Grandma, I'm glad to live here with you and Grandpa. I wouldn't like to live with a baby-sitter. I'm glad Mommy works and lets me stay here with you."*

What a saint my grandmother was! And, how wise she was to raise me in such a sheltered setting—so sheltered in fact, that I was grown before the reality truly hit me: My dad had likely married my mother "just to give me a name." I was what was referred to back in 1955 an "accident." Thankfully, my mother had been brought up to believe in the sanctity of life and so abortion was not an option—to think that I could have been another unborn child. Clearly, God wanted me here—even if she didn't! That realization, coupled with the fact that my mother was—to put it mildly—difficult, resulted in a lifelong strained relationship between my mother and me.

Mama, as she came to be known as I grew older, was the second of four children born to my grandmother and grandfather. Poor sharecroppers who rarely had enough to eat, my grandparents were unable to provide much more than a roof over their heads and the poor Southerner's diet of "beans and taters." My mother, determined to make a better life for herself, left home the week after she graduated from high school and moved to Ft. Worth to get a job.

While I'm sure I was a major "kink" in her life, Mama faithfully sent money to her mom and dad because they were taking care of me, but that money did not go for clothes, shoes or toys for me. Instead, the money she sent helped to pay the "light bill", as my grandmother called the electric bill, or to buy groceries for all of us. Despite the fact that we had so little, I never once considered leaving my grandparents; they provided me with unconditional love, safety, and a sense of being that would give me the foundation to not only survive but thrive in life.

While the decision to allow me to live with my grandparents did not seem to bother my mother any, I am so very grateful that she did not insist I come live with her when I got older. I loved school, and I flourished in small, rural Northeast Texas. Most importantly, I came to know the love of Jesus Christ and became a Christian as a young teenager. I have often wondered how I would have turned out had I been forced to move to the city with my mom. My life, although not without its difficulties, enabled me to "grow in the grace and knowledge" of our precious Lord who cares for our every concern.

Mama's and my relationship suffered all of her life. Because she was unable to communicate her thoughts and fears, her dreams and her inhibitions, our relationship stayed superficial. Despite our lack of closeness, I respected her for her independence, her tough spirit. She just didn't mean to have a daughter when she did, and she never quite learned how to be a mother. Still, I had been "raised" by my grandmother to respect my mother, and my Christian faith required that I honor my mother, and that I did. Thankfully, she, too, rededicated her life to the Lord in her latter years, and while her faith was strong, she never was able to mend the weak relationship that we had.

Then, in 2005, 33 years after having been diagnosed with ovarian cancer, and four years after having had a colostomy because of colon cancer, she heard those dreaded words, "I'm sorry; there is nothing else we can do. We recommend you allow us to call hospice." So, 50 years after giving birth to an "unwanted pregnancy", she had to come face-to-face with her mortality.

Mama died in my home on October 19, 2005, three months after she had heard those dreaded words. On her last day, I had left the sitter with her that morning and felt uneasy—she seemed different, somehow. I called in periodically during the day, and the sitter did not report anything unusual. As God would have it, I was called out of town for a few hours on my job and would be 10:00 pm before I got home. The sitter assured me that she would be there and that she would call me if she needed me. When I got home that evening and walked in the room where my mother lay in the hospital bed, I knew. The sitter had not even realized how close to dying my mother was. But, when I came in the room, she said, "Glen" and reached for my hand. I looked at her and said, "It's okay, Mom. I'm right here." Her body relaxed, but she could not speak.

God DID put me here for a reason—to be there with my mother when she passed over to meet Him; I am so glad He guides my path—and I'm so glad He was leading my mom's as well!

Anonymous

Tina Molene Creed Dulin

My heart sank as I received that frantic phone call seven years ago from my mother, telling me my 86 year-old grandmother had been rushed to the hospital with diarrhea, dehydration and severe stomach cramps. They live in Waxahachie, Texas, which is almost a seven-hour drive from Corpus Christi, where I live. Never could I have imagined losing her this way and not being able to be there for her. After all, she had survived and endured a lifetime of polio since the tender age of three.

The second call came from my mother a few hours after her arrival at Baylor Hospital there. They had found a large mass in my grandmother's pancreas and wanted additional tests for confirmation, but were giving her 6 months to live. In the morning she would be taken to "Big" Baylor, a forty-five minute drive to Dallas for further tests and treatment, however not before they were to inform my grandmother of her condition and fate. It was almost strange, in a rather comical way, to hear the anger in my mother's voice while demanding "How dare he tell my mother she only has 6 months to live!" In fact, it reminded me of how I felt as a young child sitting next to her in the Pentecostal church. Hands lifted to the sky, everyone praying aloud together while I watched her cry. These are all strong emotions that cannot be explained to anyone, much less a child. Forty years later, I know this to be "Faith."

They stabilized my grandmother and she slept well. I prayed that night and although very afraid, kept my faith and waited. Late the next morning, after her arrival to Dallas Baylor, doctors had concurred with what her local emergency room physicians had told us. They all agreed to administer a test to check again in the morning. However, due to her age, once they found what they expected, they felt she would not be able to endure the surgical procedure to remove it and still survive. Our hopes were down but our faith survived; we prayed more. She slept and felt better again that night.

Mother called the next day after the procedure and informed me that they had sedated my grandmother and found a mass in her bowel duct. However, not knowing what it was, they decided against surgical intervention due to her age. My very thankful Grandmother went home after a few days with medication and a smile on her face, as though this were a common event and nothing unusual had really happened. After she returned home, her local doctor told her she didn't need that medicine and put her on an over-the-counter treatment.

These acts are a very common occurrence for my 93-year-old grandmother to this day. In fact, I always joke that I know when she's been praying because very strange but wonderful things seem to happen, and we call this faith in the power of prayer.

Janet Leon

Even in the Little Things

Then Jesus said to his disciples: "Therefore I tell you, do not worry about your life, what you will eat; or about your body, what you will wear. Life is more than food, and the body more than clothes. Consider the ravens: They do not sow or reap, they have no store-room or barn; yet God feeds them. And how much more valuable you are than birds! Who of you by worrying can add a single hour to his life? Since you cannot do this very little thing, why do you worry about the rest?

Consider how the lilies grow. They do not labor or spin. Yet I tell you, not even Solomon in all his splendor was dressed like one of these. If that is how God clothes the grass of the field, which is here today, and tomorrow is thrown into the fire, how much more will he clothe you, O you of little faith! And do not set your heart on what you will eat or drink; do not worry about it. For the pagan world runs after all such things, and your Father knows

*that you need them. But seek his kingdom,
and these things will be given to you as well."*
Luke 12:22-31

*"And pray in the Spirit on all occasions with
all kinds of prayers and requests. With this in
mind, be alert and always keep on praying
for all the saints".* Ephesians 6:18-19

I had just started a new exercise routine of walking down the beach every morning. On my first walk, I spotted two of my husband's favorite "olive" shells, but I passed them by, thinking, "We have plenty of shells, and these are pretty rare; I'll just leave them for someone else to enjoy." Later in the day, as I told my husband about my walk, he asked if I had seen any good shells. "You left them there?" he asked, surprised and a little disappointed. I promised to bring home the next ones I spied on the beach. The next day, as I walked to the shore, I prayed, "Lord, I know every day the beach has different treasures to offer, but I would really love to delight my husband by finding those olive shells for him, if You're willing to grant me that small favor." As I retraced my steps from the day before, I noticed things had definitely been moved around by the tides and the waves, and wondered when or if I would see those perfect shells again. But it only took a few more steps before I saw not one or two, but four of the rare shells, and they were larger than those of the previous day! Instantly, I felt the joy of God's extravagant love. Not only did He bless me with what I asked for, He doubled it!

Returning home, I saw even a couple more, but I left them, as before, for someone else to enjoy. Since that day, I have walked the same stretch of beach many times, and have yet to find even one more unbroken olive shell. I know that God was answering my prayer for this small thing, reminding me that He is always listening. And if He answers little prayers like this one, I know He will hear anything and everything I ask of Him.

Donna Endicott Linnane

Prayer

Father, thank You for your extravagant love, and all the ways You remind us that You are our loving Father. Most of all, thank You for sending Jesus on our behalf. Amen.

Thought for the day

There is no prayer too great or too small for our heavenly Father.

Prayer Focus
Those who need to feel God's love and presence

Praising My God,
Axe in Hand

Over the years God has shown me time and time again the power my praises have in the spiritual realms. It's true! More and more, when times seem hopeless or someone has hurt me deeply, I just have to bust out in Praise to my God. I believe that my praises lifted up to God do more than just rattle the sound waves around me; they shake down enemy forces. It is evident in how His spirit changes my outlook, and He gives me a peace that can't be explained. I am reminded of the many outnumbered armies throughout the Old Testament who defeated their foes through their praises to God. So, I go "charging forth with praises," singing and playing my guitar. I have seen God move in mighty ways through these "weapons!"

Ephesians 6:12 says, *"For we are not fighting against people made of flesh and blood, but against the evil rulers and authorities of the unseen world, against those mighty powers of darkness who rule this world, and against wicked spirits in the heavenly realms."* I have a real enemy at work waging war against my soul. If he can distract me from my Prince of Peace, I will become self-focused and ineffective for God's kingdom. Knowing and believing this truth gives me a new perspective in every situation. When I feel as though circumstances or people are against me, I realize that focusing on me and my situation will not make things any better; it's time to praise my God. This places the focus back where it belongs. James 1:2 says, *"Dear brothers and sisters, whenever trouble comes your way, let it be an opportunity for joy."* I can't think of a better way of letting God's joy overflow in me than picking up my guitar and singing songs to Him or turning up the music loud and singing along. Now, I must admit, it's not always what I *feel* like doing. Life can really throw some doozies at me. But when I push past my feelings and I praise Him, He does bless me and that's my sacrifice of praise. *"Therefore, let us offer through Jesus a continual sacrifice of praise to God, proclaiming our allegiance to His name."* Hebrews 13:5.

These thoughts make me laugh because I know I am triumphant over my enemy through praising God. It is then that I realize how foolish I can be for not trusting that my almighty God, Creator of the universe, is bigger than anything life throws at me. He totally has my back. The laughter rises up.... it's hilarious to me to think of myself as a frightened little child clinging to the worries of this world when all along God has His hand of protection on me. It's also hilarious that the enemy really tries hard to come against this child of God, causing me to succumb to needless worry. I am not kidding myself any more. There is a very real warfare happening around me all the time. God is powerfully at work through me when I am keenly aware of it. That in itself is quite humbling, but increases my faith all the more. The Lord is my right hand... He is my avenger...my defender...my strong tower in every time of need. *"Because you are my helper, I sing for joy in the shadow of your wings."* Psalm 63:7 I will praise Him to the very end. To Him be all the glory in every circumstance!

It's funny that the slang term for a guitar is an axe. How cool is that? *"Then I will hold my head high above my enemies who surround me. At His sanctuary I will offer sacrifices with shouts of joy, singing and praising the Lord with music."* Psalm 27:6

Praising my God...axe in hand!

Sylvia Anna Madland

IF I WERE GOD

"**I**f I were God…"

Those were the words I heard my son say across the table the other night. His comment came regarding a discussion on prayer.

"If I were God, I would not let any child of mine hurt. I would not let terrorists kill innocent people. I would wipe out things like cancer. I would answer the prayers of my family. Why doesn't God do that?" he asked.

All of a sudden, years of hurt came flooding back into my spirit. Losing four family members in a plane crash is still a part of my life. Those four included my husband, my mother, my brother and my sister in-law.

Looking across the table at my son, I remembered, most of all, the pain of losing these loved ones and the fear any mother would have when left with two teen-age sons.

All four of these people loved the Lord and showed it in their lives. If God really did answer all prayers as we prayed them, those four would be standing here today.

I had reminded God of His word – "Ask and you shall receive." I told him I wanted them back, that He could resurrect them; that He could make it yesterday; that my tears were not necessary.

But that prayer was not answered.

"Where are you, God?" I had asked. Just like my son, I had wondered why God let His people suffer.

I turned to my Bible for answers. So much I just couldn't believe anymore – you know, the parts about "not allowing your foot to be moved" or "preserving you from all evil."

I searched for the scriptures I could trust.

"God created heaven and earth." OK, that was one of them. And so my study continued with my throwing out so much of what didn't seem to speak the truth. That was until I landed in Psalms.

David wrote in one verse about wishing he'd never been born and how much he was in the pit of depression. But then, in the very next verse, he would say, "Bless the Lord, oh my soul." Why was that, and how could he change his mindset so quickly?

That's when I realized David was praising God in the midst of his pain…even when he was hurting the most. The Bible tells us that God inhabits the praises of His people.

In the garden, Jesus prayed that the bitter cup He was about to partake would be removed. God did not take that pain away from Him. God knew the outcome.

I do not know why I lost my family. I cannot answer why my son's prayer was not answered in the way he wanted. But I do know God answered it. He just doesn't always say, "Yes." Sometimes He says, "No." Sometimes He says, "Wait" or "Maybe."

David, like our Lord Jesus, knew that God would work the bad for good.

My faith has catapulted me into many arenas of being called to help others in pain. I understand their grief and share my triumph over this great loss in my life. And as I tell that story, I realize that my sons and I have made it through the darkness.

God did not leave us or set out to hurt us. His plan was to make us stronger – and we are.

My son's prayer was to be successful in the music industry. Today I watched as he led the worship service for his church. His voice and music filled the room with sweet savor of prayer.

God knew how He would use him, and I knew that the prayer was already answered.

Lyn Hill

Youth in Witness

This fall, a good friend of mine felt God was calling him to go on an 11 month, 11-country mission trip. Knowing that he needed to raise a lot of money, and that God wanted him to do it, he sold everything he had — car, iPod, CDs — everything, to raise money for the trip. Unfortunately, he still needed $6,000 to go. Confident that God would provide, he put off asking for money until the last week. On a Thursday, he sent an email to all of his friends saying that he needed to raise $6,000 by Monday. The thing was that, since he grew up in a Jewish family and had only become a Christian a few years before; he had no home church and had no support from his family. But, God provided. In that one weekend, he was able to raise over $6,000 just from friends who know God was going to work through him on this intense mission trip. Currently, he is still on the trip sharing the love of God with Russians. He has already been all over Africa, China, and South America. This is a great example of God providing for what He has called us to do. It may seem that God asked a lot of him — selling everything he owned — but it is no comparison to the amazing things he has been able to do in the name of the Lord.

Anonymous

Youth in Witness

Taylor,

I have always had trouble with staying away from home alone. When I would go to Boy Scout Camps or even when I went to CAC, I have had trouble feeling comfortable. This summer I am going to a Boy Scout camp in New Mexico and CAC alone.

My dad broke his heel last week and my mom can't go with me to CAC. She has to stay behind and help him. The camp in New Mexico is 7 days long. Plus, we will stay somewhere for the night the way up and down. That is 9 nights total! I have never stayed from home longer than 1 night without being completely alone (by that I mean no family).

All this is going to be a huge obstacle for me to overcome. The reason I am going is because God has given me the strength, although I still feel a little nervous and sometimes disagree with going. However I overcame this by remembering the fun times that I have had at camps without my parents or sister being there. I also focus on the one true thing

– GOD WILL BE BY MY SIDE! He will be there all the way.

Taylor, I know that you will make it through this and you will be just fine. God cares for you so much and he will help you. I pray that all the love that family and friends have spread around you will keep you comfortable and the grace of God will carry you through this.
God loves you! Don't forget it!

Love,
Aaron Clark

Youth in Witness

This summer, I have been so incredibly blessed to be working at First United Methodist Church as a youth intern. Coming in to this experience, I was coasting through in my relationship with the Lord, becoming impatient at his apparent lack of response to my prayers. The fact that I couldn't see His hand in my life was frustrating for me. My freshman year of college had NOT gone according to plan. My longtime friend and roommate for my first semester and I were no longer friends, in fact we pretty much loathed each other, I had gone through about 5 potential changes of my major, and I wasn't getting too far on that MRS (you know, Mrs.? yeah I know, it's not that funny) degree I was hoping to acquire. So quite frankly, I was irritated with God. I'm a fairly constant person, I don't really accept change well, and this year was absolutely FULL of changes.

I came home for the summer, loving the idea of working as an intern. I love my youth group and there isn't a better job in the world for me because I love working with kids — I always have. I was living with the mindset that it was my job to be a good example for the youth. I mean, that's what I was getting paid for, right? As imperfect as I am, I figured that if I'm just as good as I can be, then it'll all be okay. But then a funny thing started happening. I started watching the students and their growing faith and suddenly, they were the ones setting the example for me. I was humbled and definitely awed. From that first week on, my faith has solidified into something more than I had ever hoped for it to be. Jesus literally became the foundation of my life. He came back up to center stage in my life instead of being shoved into a corner.

I look back now on my freshman year of college and I can see God's hand in my life. It's so painfully obvious that I'm shocked that I couldn't see it before. He was just letting me try things my way and gently leading me down His path through my experiments. Jesus has never abandoned me, and He never will. I still don't know where I'm going, but as long as I know Who I'm following, I know I'll be okay.

Although God isn't as direct as I would like Him to be with His plan for my life, I'm learning to trust. Being in control of my life is something that I had become accustomed to, and it's hard to let that go, but I'm working on it. I'm nowhere near perfect and I never will be, but Jesus loves me anyway and I know that He will provide for my life. He will make His plan known, but only when I have fully and completely surrendered my life to Him. He knows what my major should be, He knows which friends will stick around for the rest of my life, and He also knows who I will marry. But I have to find my joy in Him before He will reveal it.

Taylor, I'm praying for you and I know that God has much much MUCH more in store for your life. You are so great and I'm planning on seeing you at CAC next year! Keep that bright smile on your face. We love you!

Jill Moore

Youth in Witness

I've always been a shy person. Conversation-starting is not my forte and I'm not one to just walk up to a group of people I don't know well and join in. When I began going to youth group in 6th grade, I struggled to find friends and fit in with a group of girls. There weren't many other girls my age that went, and so it took a couple of years until I really was comfortable at every youth event. I'm not outgoing, and I always admired the college interns every summer because they were. It seemed they could lead any group, start a conversation with anyone, and just make anybody feel welcome and loved.

As I grew older, I began to be a leader in the youth group. But even then, speaking in front of people or meeting someone new took all the courage I had. I knew I had to rely on Jesus through it all, and He gave me strength when I needed it. Yet I still felt terrified anytime I prayed out loud, talked at worship, or reached out to a new student. I was certain there was no way God could push me any farther in this area of my faith. But, of course, God had way more amazing plans than I could have imagined then.

During the summer before my junior year in high school, I was going to be a counselor at our junior high camp. I felt comfortable about the job, since I had experience from the year before, and I was sure I could handle it. And then, I was asked to help lead worship at camp. Not only did that require me to stand in front of people with a microphone, but I had to sing too! Sure, I could carry a tune fairly well, but I was no singer, and wouldn't even sing at home in front of my family. I prayed about the position a lot, and reluctantly was forced to admit that this was something God was calling me to do. But He also gave me the strength and encouragement I needed to do it. He gave me supportive family and friends, who lifted me up and encouraged me when I thought I couldn't keep going. And I kept leading worship through the entire school year too. Never would I have ever guessed I would ever sing in front of other people. But God also reminded me that we don't have to sound like professionals to please Him, but it's about our hearts and our attitude. As long as we are completely focused on Him, He wouldn't ask for any more.

But God still wasn't done. Towards the end of my junior year, my youth director approached me with the idea of being a "junior intern" that summer. Normally, interns were college-age or at least going into college, but when the school year came around, they left, and it was hard to just cut off the relationships the students had made with the interns. He asked me to pray about the opportunity and just see where God wanted me this summer. I was very unsure about it all. I didn't feel mature enough in my faith, or responsible enough, or ready. I hadn't planned on this at all, and I knew it would only work if God were working through me. So I prayed a lot about what His plan was, and asked that He would fill me with courage and enthusiasm about interning if that was where He wanted me. As May approached, I began to be excited about the idea of getting to plan the events for the summer and building relationships with the students. I accepted the offer to be a junior intern, and while it's definitely been challenging and trying, I know God is giving me the strength to get through each week. It's still not something that I feel fits me, but it forces me to rely on Jesus and allow Him to use me as His tool.

God tends to have plans for us that we wouldn't ever choose for ourselves, but because of that, we have to rely on Him more. Trusting God with our lives is hard, and it's not necessarily comfortable, but it results in the life we were created to live, and nothing we plan could ever be better.

Allison Clark

Youth in Witness

As I look back on my life, I can clearly see the hand of God guiding me, changing me, challenging me. But this past year, I have felt closer to Jesus than ever before in my life. Honestly, I believe that is because I am finally beginning to trust Him with everything. For my first year in college, it was pretty rough. I chose to go to a school not because I wanted to or because my friends were there, but because I felt that's where God wanted me. The first semester wasn't so much fun. I didn't know anyone. I was a part of a grueling scholarship program that demanded a lot of my time in addition to 15 hours of my first college semester. I felt out of place at a catholic and predominately Hispanic school and refused to call my dorm room home. Yet God was there. When I freaked out about a problem with my schedule the first week of classes, He worked it out the next day in the best possible way. When I nervously drove up the on ramp to merge onto the San Antonio freeway the first time by myself, He cleared all 4 lanes. When I missed my Christian family so bad my heart ached,

He loved me through the people in my new church and renewed my strength in worship. When I longed for the encouragement and comfort of praying with others, He worked through one of my new friends and pastors who talked to Jesus with me. Over and over again, I saw Him in everything I did. No matter how much I hurt, He was there. He was faithful. And He proved that He is the only one worthy of my trust. When I missed getting hugs from my mom and laughing with my best friend, when I missed walking into a room and having everyone know me and be excited to see me, Jesus was the one who filled me up. He was the one who wiped away my tears and wrapped me up in His love. And slowly, as I put my trust in Him, He showed me opportunities. He showed me the reason that this was in His plan for me. I was able to pour my heart out to my unbelieving room-mates and be honest and open about the amazing God I worship. I was able to completely be myself around the other students in the scholarship program and was not afraid to clearly stand for Jesus. I was able to love and serve the students in my classes and give God the glory for any good thing that came my way. Oh, I still messed up, I still turned away from Jesus, tried to take back control, worried, and tried to find comfort in other people, but no matter what, God never gave up on me. His faithfulness overcame my fear and my sadness. Since the beginning of my second semester, I can honestly say that I love my college. I love being there because that's where God wants me to be. I love being there because He has brought me amazing friends who I pray will come to know the indescribable love and power of our God. For the first time in my life, I can feel God speaking to me. He guided me so that this summer I followed His plan. He has given me words and ideas and a passion to be able to do His work and I'm to the point that I no longer know how to praise Him because He is so, so good to me. His love knows NO limits. And above all, he is WORTHY of our trust. so even now, when I think about the future, how there are so many hurdles to overcome, how unknown the next few years and my career are, I don't have to worry, or try to work everything out in a spreadsheet, or give up because it just seems too impossible, I can trust in His plan. When I think about the fact that I am 19 years old and have never had a boyfriend, I don't have to sit here and ask God why this hasn't happened for me or doubt that He has created me beautifully and wonderfully, I can trust that He is in control, that He will give me the desires of my heart if I commit my way to Him. So I trust. I hope. I live in Him. And that is the only place I ever want to be. Our God is faithful. His love is strong. When He says He will never leave us nor forsake us, He means it. I live with the confidence that God is bigger than going to college, He's bigger than anything the world can throw at us; He is leading me; He is here with me, and that is enough for me.

Sara Wilkinson

The Plan of Salvation

"Create in me a new heart"

"For all have sinned and fallen short of the glory of God" Romans 3:23

We have all sinned and yet somehow we skim over the words in Romans 3:23. There is nothing harder than to look at oneself with critical eyes; to look at the deep dark places of our lives and see them through God's eyes. It's much easier to judge ourselves according to worldly standards. Because we always seem to be able to find someone we think is worse than ourselves.

God knows all those deep and dark places we hide. He knows your heart. Psalm 33:15 declares, *"He creates the hearts of all people. He is aware of everything they do"*. And He still loves us.

God's heart for us is so incredibly overflowing with love. Even when we are neck deep in sin, God is there. He has known you from the beginning of time. He knows all your failures and He still wants to be in relationship with you. It is His plan that we should all be forever with Him, to experience that amazing grace He so freely offers. If you are willing, He is ready to take you where you are and give you a new heart.

Just pray! Lord, I see now that I am a sinner. That it is impossible for me to be anything else without You in my life. That You love me so much You sent your Son Jesus to die on a cross; a sacrifice for my sin. I want to honor that sacrifice with the rest of my life. I submit to you as Lord of my life. Come with your sanctifying grace and transform my heart anew. Amen.

If you prayed that prayer, you are now and forever a child of the Most High. Continue to seek His face in His Word. Find a church home where they teach the Bible, and love and encourage you in obedience to that Word. Life will continue to have its ups and downs but now you have in you the Hope of life eternal with the Father that is Alpha and Omega, the First and the Last and He will continue from now to eternity to touch your new heart in ways you never imagined.

God, create a pure heart in me. Give me a
new spirit that is faithful to you.
Psalm 51:10

Thank You

Among these pages you have seen the miracles of many, the tears of joy seen when one waits upon the Lord, and the beauty of walking closely with a Father who loves you and is never to busy to sit and chat awhile. You have found strength, hope, and an unconditional love poured out in times of happiness, pain, and long walks in the valley.

What a beautiful gift our heavenly Father has given our community through each of our struggles, joys, and personal walk with Christ. I am especially honored to have this project benefit Taylor's Heart Transplant Foundation. When Taylor was first diagnosed with Restrictive Cardiomyopathy a friend came to us and said "I had a dream that God would use Taylor in a mighty way to spread his word." She was given the Scripture 2 Kings 20. King Hezekiah was very ill. He had been told by Isaiah that he would not recover. King Hezekiah cried out to the Lord, reminding God of how faithful and devoted he had been. God sent Isaiah back to tell Hezekiah to tell him that He had heard his prayer and seen his tears;

He would heal him. And he was then to go up to the temple of the Lord. The Lord through this passage showed her that Taylor would be healed and would some day stand in the temple of the Lord and declare God's mercy and glory.

I can think of no better way to be used by God than to have our Christian brothers and sisters standing with us in faith, sharing personal testimonies of how a majestic God has worked in their lives.

I give a personal thanks to all for your prayers, your financial support of this book, and the opportunity to live a long and full life.

May God Bless You!

The Berry Family

Lightning Source UK Ltd.
Milton Keynes UK
04 December 2009

165780LV00001B/2/P